PRACTITIONER'S GUIDE TO ECONOMIC DEVELOPMENT FINANCE
– BUILDING AND UTILIZING THE DEVELOPMENT FINANCE TOOLBOX –
BY TOBY RITTNER

Lee Chilcote
Editor

85 East Gay Street, Suite 700
Columbus, Ohio 43215
www.cdfa.net

CDFA would like to thank the many individuals and organizations that have assisted in the development of this publication. In particular, CDFA thanks the professionals who have assisted in providing content for the various chapters and case studies including:

CDFA Board of Directors

Chairman
Rick Palank
St. Louis County
Economic Council

Treasurer
James Parks
Louisiana Public
Facilities Authority

Vice-Chairman
Darnell Moses
Allegheny County Economic Development

Secretary
John Kerr
Detroit/Wayne County Port Authority

Maureen Babis
New York City Economic
Development Corporation

Mark Huston
Cimarron Capital Partners, LLC

Frank Bordeaux
North Carolina Agricultural Finance Authority

Steve Johnson
Colorado Housing and
Finance Authority

Jo Bradley
Vermont Economic Development Authority

Bob Lind
City of Minneapolis

Joseph Branca
Banc of America Securities LLC

Eileen Marxen
California Industrial Development Financing Advisory
Commission

Steve Chilton
MassDevelopment

Brian McMahon
New York State
Economic Development Council

John Doherty
U.S. Bank

Tina Neal
Piper Jaffray

Gene Eagle
Arkansas Development Finance Authority

Ken Powell
Stone & Youngberg LLC

Charlie Emmons
Finance Authority of Maine

Laura Radcliff
Stifel Nicolaus

John Filan
Illinois Finance Authority

Wyatt Shiflett
Maryland Department of Business
& Economic Development

Caren Franzini
New Jersey Economic Development Authority

Jeff Freese
KeyBanc Capital Markets

Gary Smith
Chester County Industrial
Development Authority

Peter Glick
Wells Fargo Brokerage Services, Inc.

Cheryl Strickland
Atlanta Development Authority

Dan Harrison
California Statewide Communities
Development Authority

John Wahrgren
Oregon Economic and
Community Development Department

Marc Hughes
Jefferies & Co., Inc.

Frances Walton
Empire State Development Corporation

CDFA General Counsel

Arthur Cohen
Hawkins Delafield & Wood LLP

Case Studies Contributors

- City of Minneapolis Department of Community Planning and Economic Development
- Atlanta Development Authority
- City/County of Denver Office of Economic Development, Denver Urban Redevelopment Authority
- Allegheny County Economic Development
- St. Louis County Economic Council
- Chester County Economic Development Council
- New Jersey Economic Development Authority
- MassDevelopment
- Arkansas Development Finance Authority
- Oregon Economic and Community Development Department

Case Studies
Brian Anderson

Editor
Lee Chilcote

Proofreader
Jill Riga

Project Management
Katie Kramer

Photo Credit: Chris Holley-Starling

Toby Rittner is the President and CEO of the Council of Development Finance Agencies (CDFA). He runs the day-to-day operations of the Council, which includes management of a 32 member Board of Directors, and the organization's various educational, advocacy and research initiatives. Rittner is a frequent speaker at local, state and national conferences and events focused on economic development finance. He has been featured extensively in The Bond Buyer and other national media publications concerning the advancement of development finance tools.

Rittner has advised numerous local, state and federal government leaders, including President Obama's Transition Team, on economic development finance policy and practices.

Prior to joining CDFA, Rittner was the Director of Legislative Affairs and former Director of Training for the International Economic Development Council (IEDC). Rittner has also worked for the Franklin County, Ohio Board of Commissioners, Community and Economic Development Department as a Senior Program Coordinator for Economic Development and as an Associate Planner for the City of Gahanna, Ohio.

Rittner is a Certified Economic Development Finance Professional (EDFP) through the National Development Council (NDC) and serves on the Board of Directors for the Mid-America Economic Development Council (MAEDC). Rittner is also an appointed member of the City of Cleveland Heights Citizens Advisory Committee and a Board Member of FutureHeights, a non-profit organization addressing community and economic development locally. Rittner holds a Bachelor of Arts in Political Science and a Master's of City and Regional Planning degree from The Ohio State University.

As the economic development industry has evolved, a large number of agencies have expanded their focus to include everything from business and industry attraction and retention to development and redevelopment. Establishing a comprehensive financing program to assist in these efforts is critical, yet, despite this, recognition of the development finance toolbox has been slow to emerge. This has left many communities struggling to understand the complexities of development finance and often apprehensive to implement many critical tools.

CDFA is proud to release this book as the industry's first "practitioner's guide" for building and utilizing the development finance toolbox. It is the first step in a broad-based initiative by CDFA to educate the economic development industry and thousands of community leaders on the expanse of potential financing options available to encourage development, job growth, investment and sustainability.

I spent the better part of a year researching the myriad of financing tools that exist, and, while I recognize that not every potential financing tool is included, I believe that this book offers the most comprehensive look at the development finance toolbox. The toolbox approach is being used by a variety of economic development agencies to wide acclaim and great success, and I have highlighted many of these successful agencies in the book. I hope that the case studies in Chapter 8 will inspire agencies of all sizes to implement this philosophy.

Several individuals were instrumental in producing this book. In particular, I would like to thank the dedicated members of the CDFA Board of Directors, Brian Anderson from the CDFA team, and my editor Lee Chilcote. Finally, I owe a very special thank you to Katie Kramer for her patience with me while managing this project.

Toby Rittner, EDFP
President & CEO
Council of Development Finance Agencies

What is Development Finance?

Development finance is the effort of local communities to support, encourage and catalyze economic growth. It is a tool to help make a project or deal successful, and in turn, to create a benefit for the long-term health of a community. This benefit is the economic growth that can take place through public and private investment in infrastructure, business and industry.

Development finance offers a potential solution to the challenges of the local economic, business and industrial environment. To use development finance tools effectively, practitioners must possess an understanding of the myriad programs, resources and terminology that exist in this field.

Economic development professionals play an important role as the bridge between government and business. They direct the use of precious public resources, inform policy decisions about how resources are allocated, and act as catalysts for important projects.

What Does Development Finance Include?

Development finance tools come in a variety of forms. These tools include loans, equity, tax abatements and tax credits. They also include the offer of a guarantee, collateral or some other form of credit enhancement within the context of a complex financing package. Development finance may include gap financing, which often makes the difference between a project that is contemplated, and one that reaches fruition. Development finance tools may also include the remediation of environmental concerns, as well as incentives, grants or other resources for businesses and entrepreneurs.

Development finance is a proactive approach towards finance intended to assist economic development projects. It leverages valuable public resources to support significant private sector investment. In doing so, development finance helps to solve the needs of business, industry, developers and investors, while also contributing to a community's long-term health and goals.

What Does Development Finance Not Include?

Development finance comes with accountability measures, and it is not a "free ride" for businesses in need of assistance. The use of public resources should be tied to performance measures and project achievements. Development finance programs should not compete with programs offered by private financial institutions, because this could create conflict, an uneven playing field and a lack of cooperation among stakeholders. Rather, public financing should complement and enhance the offerings of the private sector.

Public contributions towards development finance should bring commensurate public rewards. Unabashed subsidies that provide public contribution while requiring too little private commitment are not considered good practice by professionals.

Balancing public risk against public reward is perhaps the most difficult component of this process. However, development professionals have established methodologies to determine the appropriate amount of public financing that should be contributed to a project or a business. Such methodologies help the public to achieve a maximum return on its investment.

Development finance requires a rational, thoughtful and strategic response to economic needs and challenges. Many communities struggle with sudden economic adjustments due to plant closings, corporate relocations, or business expansions. Community leaders are placed under considerable pressure to address these challenges quickly. To present a thoughtful response to such challenges, development finance must include long-term, strategic thinking.

Why is Development Finance Important?

Development finance is critical to economic development because it has the potential to make or break a project. Businesses need access to financial resources to complete a project or deal. Whether the funds are used for site acquisition or start-up capital, nearly all projects hinge on the borrower's ability to leverage convenient sources of financing. Development finance may offer a type of financing that is less expensive than conventional, private financing.

Development finance can help businesses to generate working capital and invest in their ideas. It can help developers achieve an acceptable return on investment (ROI) in a given project. It can help communities to develop infrastructure, jobs and amenities. In pursuing a development finance strategy, it is essential to balance the needs of industry with the needs of the community.

A proposal to use development finance tools may act as a catalyst for development led by the private sector, regardless of whether or not public financing is actually utilized. For instance, the creation of a tax increment financing district (TIF) can cause an increase in investment based on the speculation that real estate values will increase in this area – even if the municipality never issues a bond or finances a deal. Such increased investment may cause real estate values to rise, thus bringing in additional tax revenues in areas targeted for redevelopment. And, the increase in investment spurred by the use or perceived use of development finance tools may ultimately help to foster community buy-in.

Trends in Development Finance

The development finance industry ebbs and flows with the economy, and is often subject to the same market forces as traditional lending tools. Development finance agencies take on a variety of roles, including:

- Issuing bonds directly, or acting as a conduit issuer
- Providing direct loans
- Providing loan guarantees or other collateral support
- Providing grants
- Providing technical assistance
- Serving as developer or development partner

Despite all of this, according to CDFA research, 50% of all finance agencies allocate less than 20% of their actual budget to financing development.

There are a variety of reasons for this, including the complexity of programs, lack of staff education and a general lack of resources for administering programs. In the most extreme cases, a lack of political support for certain tools also exists.

Development finance is a complex undertaking. These tools require a considerable amount of knowledge and training, and in many communities the resources to educate all of the parties involved do not exist. Lack of education and training is a major hindrance to the development finance process, and it can create project obstacles and cause legal problems in the long run.

Education is the most critical strategy to make these tools easier to use and understand. Successful agencies build their programs by educating staff and leadership. Because education requires an investment of resources, development finance agencies must be mindful of allocating funds for this purpose.

Public or Public/Private?

The structure of a development finance agency can play a major role in its success. Public agencies, such as city and county departments of development, provide one approach. In larger communities, these agencies are often directed by municipal employees, while in smaller communities, they are often managed by mayors or city managers. These agencies provide a set of conventional public financing tools that are both tested and reliable. Yet public agencies, by their nature, lack more innovative financing programs. They often cannot offer comprehensive financing options or provide great depth in financing. Furthermore, they are sometimes hindered by budget constraints and frequent changes in political leadership.

Public/private agencies provide another approach to development finance. These agencies are typically governed by a board of appointed members that represent various stakeholder groups in the community. Through statute, ordinance or other legal means, these agencies are given powers to issue debt, enter into agreements, and provide direct financing to business and industry on behalf of local governments. Public/private agencies may also have the ability to work outside of traditional governmental boundaries. They can provide a depth of financing that is comparable to the private sector.

Types of financing provided by public/private agencies may include seed or venture capital for small businesses, loan funds, and an array of investment tools not generally used by public agencies. Public/private agencies must typically compete for funding. They are often supported by local communities with direct funding, and also through fees for services, bond issuances and development agreements. The limitations of public/private agencies include less government oversight and the danger of decisions becoming politically charged.

There is an argument to be made for the effectiveness of both public and public/private agencies. However, CDFA research shows that public/private structures tend to provide a greater breadth and depth of financing resources at the local level. In a CDFA survey of hundreds of agencies, 81% of the public agencies indicated that they allocated less than 20% of their budget directly to development finance, whereas 33% of public/private agencies allocate over 50% of their budget to development finance. This disparity indicates that public/private agencies may be better equipped to provide development finance options.

The Financing Spectrum

Every economic development transaction presents different challenges. For instance, large-scale industrial development requires a different financing approach when compared to small business development. Typically, development finance is broken down into a spectrum of approaches. Having an understanding of this spectrum will allow development finance agencies to address the needs of established industries, large real estate development projects, small businesses, and individual entrepreneurs.

Some financing options, such as a revolving loan fund, may address a variety of needs and clients. To be effective, however, most development finance efforts must be tailored to a specific need or project. For instance, real estate development does not require the use of start-up capital such as seed or venture capital funding. On the other hand, an early stage entrepreneur is not likely to benefit from bond financing.

This guide will explore the spectrum of development finance tools. Understanding this spectrum is critical to maximizing the development finance resources available in a community.

Development Finance SPECTRUM

Types of Financings

	Government Projects	Established Industry	Development & Redevelopment	Small Business & Micro-Enterprises	Entrepreneurs
Practice Areas					

BEDROCK TOOLS

TARGETED TOOLS

INVESTMENT TOOLS

ACCESS TO CAPITAL LENDING TOOLS

SUPPORT TOOLS

From the Practitioner's Guide to Economic Development Finance

THE PRACTITIONER'S GUIDE TO ECONOMIC DEVELOPMENT FINANCE

CHAPTER 2
BUILDING THE
DEVELOPMENT FINANCE TOOLBOX

Introducing the Toolbox Approach

Hundreds of development finance programs exist at the federal, state and local level. These programs have been created over the past two centuries to address the financing needs of business, industry, real estate, housing, environmental and community development entities. Individually, none of these programs are a silver bullet solution to economic development challenges that such entities face.

The toolbox approach to development finance brings together the best of these financing concepts and techniques to provide a comprehensive response to capital and resource needs. The toolbox approach offers programs and resources that harness the full spectrum of financing options. This approach requires a commitment to public/private partnerships, and the creation of niche programs to assist different types of industries and enterprises. Whether assisting large-scale industrial development projects or small, micro-enterprise business development, the toolbox approach is designed to help numerous types of users, and to maximize opportunities for growth in the local economy.

Why the Toolbox Approach?

Economic development professionals have one of the most difficult jobs in local government: to catalyze investment, to promote opportunity for new and expanding businesses, and to create jobs. The toolbox approach recognizes the financing challenges that are faced by economic development projects, and seeks to provide realistic and comprehensive solutions.

A broad array of financing programs currently exists across the country, yet in most cases, these programs are under-utilized. The use of tax credit programs is an example. According to CDFA research, less than five percent of finance agencies frequently employ the use of state and federal tax credit programs. Yet these tax credit programs represent the most abundant financing source in the country, offering targeted and tailored programs to address financing needs.

Using the toolbox approach allows economic development professionals to take a comprehensive approach to financing. The toolbox pulls together a variety of programs, and offers different tools for a range of users and projects. The toolbox also collects funding sources at the federal, state and local government level, and within the private sector, in one place. This comprehensive approach towards the use of public resources is one that is more likely to attract business, investment and growth to a community.

The Toolbox and Financing Spectrum

Understanding the development finance spectrum is critical to maximizing the resources available in a community. The toolbox approach addresses this spectrum by breaking down dozens of financing options into five practice areas:

Practice Area 1: Bedrock Tools
Bonds and the Basics of Public Finance

Practice Area 2: Targeted Tools
Tax Increment Finance, Special Assessment Districts, Government Districts and Project Specific District Financing

Practice Area 3: Investment Tools
Tax Credits, Seed & Venture Capital and Angel Funds

Practice Area 4: Access to Capital Lending Tools
Revolving Loan Funds, Mezzanine Funds, Loan Guarantees and Microenterprise Finance

Practice Area 5: Support Tools
Federal Economic Development Programs and Tax Abatements

Though not all financing programs fall neatly within these five practice areas, the toolbox approach is designed to provide a more efficient and effective process for addressing financing needs. The toolbox approach also allows economic development professionals the opportunity to test a variety of strategies on a given project, and to combine programs in order to address financing needs.

Public Policy Goals

It is important that the programs in the toolbox adhere to broader public policy goals, and that they allocate precious public resources efficiently. By making programs available to businesses and individuals, a development agency is indicating that these tools have been fully vetted, developed and prepared for use, and that they comply with the guidelines and goals of the agency.

In the field of economic development, the financing of development projects can ultimately impact public policy. When public resources are used to finance projects, the success of these projects is likely to drive future public financing and policy considerations. This is perhaps most critical in urban communities seeking the financial capacity to support redevelopment. By bringing together a variety of parties – including banks, thrifts, educational providers, investors, angels and developers – the toolbox approach may help to expand a community's capacity to take on new economic development projects.

Understanding Bedrock Tools

Bonds are the bedrock of public development finance. They have been used to help build roads, bridges, sewers, dams, city halls, prisons, schools, hospitals, libraries and thousands of other public and private projects. Though bonds date back to the 19th century, the tax reform of 1986 helped to shape the way communities use bonds today.

To understand and employ the tools of development finance, practitioners must understand the basics of bond finance. This subject is very complex, and using these tools requires considerable oversight and due diligence. In order to be used properly, public and private development finance agencies must employ qualified professionals, and offer appropriate training and education.

The Basics of Bond Finance

In its simplest form, a bond is a debt or a loan incurred by a governmental entity. The bonds are issued and sold to the investing public, and the proceeds are typically made available to finance the costs of a capital project. If the bonds are being issued for the benefit of a non-governmental borrower, the proceeds are often loaned to such borrower, and the borrower then makes loan payments corresponding to when principal and interest are due on the bonds.

Each bondholder receives interest over the term of the bonds, and such interest is often exempt from federal income taxes and state and local income taxes. The tax-exempt status of certain bonds makes them an attractive investment option for investors.

Types of Bonds

There are two types of bonds: Governmental Bonds and Private Activity Bonds (PABs). The interest that accrues on Governmental Bonds and "Qualified PABs" is exempt from federal taxation. Unlike Qualified PABs, Governmental Bonds may be used for many public purposes (e.g., highways, schools, bridges, sewers, jails, parks, government equipment and buildings, etc.). Private entities may not significantly use, operate, control or own the facilities that are being financed. Governmental Bonds benefit the general public, while PABs benefit private entities. Governmental Bonds are intended to address an "essential government function" such as building a highway or a school.

A bond issuer's objective is to raise capital at the lowest cost. The tax-exempt treatment of Governmental Bonds makes them the lowest cost option. However, various "private activity tests" serve to limit the amount of private sector involvement with facilities that are financed with Governmental Bonds.

On the other hand, qualified PABs permit a larger degree of private sector involvement, but they do so at a higher interest rate. In the economic development industry, Qualified PABs are the development finance mechanisms that drive projects involving both the public and private sector.

Economic Development Bond Use

PABs may be used to address numerous economic development finance needs. They are issued for the benefit of private entities. The Internal Revenue Code (IRC) permits the financing of several types of facilities using qualified PABs, although they may be used partially or entirely for private purposes:

Small Issue Industrial Development Bonds (IDBs)

Bonds in this category include Industrial Development Bonds (IDBs), which are often referred to as Small Issue Manufacturing Bonds. These bonds are the single most actively used bond tool for financing the manufacturing industry. IDBs are issued for qualified manufacturing projects, with a total bond issuance limit of ten million dollars. These bonds can support expansion and investment in existing manufacturing facilities, as well as the development of new facilities and the purchase of new machinery and equipment.

Aggie Bonds

The category of qualified, small issue bonds also includes a type of bond used for first-time farmers. These bonds are called Aggie Bonds. Aggie Bond programs, which exist in numerous states, help to support agricultural investment. These bonds provide an attractive, affordable source of capital for first-time farmers looking to invest in a new business venture. Aggie Bond programs are generally run by the state agriculture department or a similar authority.

501(c)(3) Bonds for Not-For-Profits

This category of bond is used to finance projects owned and used by not-for-profit corporations who have received a determination letter from the Internal Revenue Service (IRS) that they qualify as exempt under Section 501(c)(3) of the IRC. Due to the relative affordability of this type of financing, 501(c)(3) bonds have gained in popularity over the past several years. There are two types of qualified 501(c)(3) bonds, "qualified hospital bonds" and "qualified non-hospital bonds." The latter type are often used for educational and charitable institutions. Organizations using Qualified 501(c)(3) bonds may include: religious or charitable groups, scientific organizations, literary or educational groups, and others. 501(c)(3) bonds are not subject to state volume cap requirements.

Exempt Facility Bonds

This category of bonds may be used to finance a wide variety of projects, including airports, docks and wharves, mass-commuting facilities (such as high-speed rail) and water and sewage facilities. Exempt Facility Bonds may also be used to help finance solid waste disposal facilities, qualified residential rental projects, facilities for the furnishing of electric energy or gas and facilities for local district heating and cooling. These bonds may also be used for qualified hazardous waste facilities, environmental enhancements of hydroelectric generating facilities, qualified public educational facilities, qualified green building and sustainable design projects, and qualified highway or surface freight transfer facilities. Exempt Facility Bonds have a very wide scope of use, and implementation varies by state or local community.

Qualified Redevelopment Bonds

Infrastructure projects the financing for which does not meet the IRC requirements for Governmental Bonds may qualify for tax exempt financing if they meet several tests for "qualified redevelopment bonds." For instance, in many cases, the proceeds must be used for redevelopment in designated areas of blight. These bonds are typically issued for projects that involve special district financing, such as tax increment financing.

Enterprise Zone Bonds

Enterprise Zone Bonds may be issued for projects in federally designated enterprise or empowerment zone communities. If certain tests are met, bond proceeds may be used to finance projects for commercial and manufacturing facilities.

Qualified Mortgage Bonds

This is the single-family mortgage revenue bond program that makes available below-market interest rate mortgages to first-time homebuyers. There is also a qualified veteran's mortgage bond program with similar characteristics.

New Clean Renewable Energy Bonds (New CREB's)

CREB's are a new form of tax credit bond that have recently been updated by the federal government and dubbed as New CREBs. New CREBs may be used to finance certain qualified renewable energy facilities that produce electricity. The facilities must be owned by public power providers (PPPs), governmental bodies (including Indian tribal governments), or mutual or cooperative electric companies (CECs). Under the New CREBs program, 100% of the available project proceeds (i.e. at least 98% of the sale proceeds) must be spent on capital expenditures incurred by PPPs, CECs or governmental bodies. When using these bonds, the holder of the New CREB receives a federal tax credit in lieu of tax-exempt interest paid by the issuer. New CREBs are intended to allow qualified issuers and qualified borrowers to borrow at a 0% interest rate or close thereto. Depending on the holder's tax bracket, the federal tax benefit to the holder of a New CREB may be greater than the benefit derived from tax-exempt interest on municipal bonds because the tax credit derived from a New CREB can be used to offset, on a dollar-for-dollar basis, a holder's current-year tax liability (including AMT liability). Unlike tax-exempt bonds, New CREBs are taxable bonds, and the tax credits that are received are treated as interest and included within a bondholder's taxable income before they are applied to offset it.

Qualified Energy Conservation Bonds (QECBs)
QECBs are another form of tax credit bond where the bondholder receives payments in the form of tax credits from the federal government. The tax credits permit an issuer of a QECB potentially to borrow for "qualified conservation purposes" at much lower interest rates. "Qualified conservation purposes" may include a wide variety of opportunities, from capital expenditures for renewable energy source development, energy consumption reduction and green program development, to facility and research grants. The wide variety of financing opportunities with QECBs makes the program very flexible and popular and should be explored by communities working to develop green and renewable energy initiatives

Qualified Zone Academy Bonds (QZABs)
The Qualified Zone Academy Bond is another federal tax credit bond program. QZABs may be used for most school renovation and rehabilitation projects as well as equipment and up-to-date technology. New construction does not qualify. Through the tax credit, the federal government covers, on average, all of the interest on these bonds, thus school jurisdictions do not have to pay interest on the bonds, which results in substantial savings. The bondholder receives a federal tax credit instead of interest. The maturity of the bond cannot exceed 50% of the present value of the principal amount borrowed, or 12-16 years. School districts qualify for QZAB financing if they reasonably expect at least 35% of their student body will qualify for the free or reduced lunch program. Also, individual schools can qualify even if their district does not. To participate in the program, schools must have "substantial business support." This means written commitments (matching funds) of not less than 10% of the proposed project from a private sector partner. Development agencies often help to identify partners or act as composite issuers.

Creative Bond Programs
Understanding the scope of PABs and how they can be used for economic development is only the first part of utilizing the development finance toolbox. Many finance agencies have capitalized on the availability of PABs by building programs that are specifically designed to capture these benefits for a wider audience.

Mini Bond Programs
Traditionally, bond programs target larger businesses and users. To address the capital needs of smaller users, and to make bond financing more accessible, many agencies have created Mini Bond Programs. Such programs may significantly lower the upfront and annual fees on tax-exempt issuances by providing a

streamlined application process, standardized documents, and a reduction in the number of industry professionals involved. Less red tape translates into lower costs for the borrower. Take IDBs, for instance – the application and approval process for conventional IDBs can take up to six months or more, require detailed documentation, and necessitate involvement of bond professionals. Mini Bond Programs are more convenient for smaller users.

During the Mini Bond application process, businesses must demonstrate excellent financial standing and provide sufficient collateral. Additional evaluation criteria are established by the local authority. Professional fees, which can make smaller deals less economical, are reduced. The need for a placement agent, re-marketing agent, letter of credit bank (with associated legal fees), rating, and bond trustee is reduced or eliminated. While bond pricing may be higher, it is offset by lower fees, which may have a significant impact on the cost of borrowing.

The use of a Mini Bond Program is just one example of how a smaller development finance agency may be able to implement a strong bond program while limiting the investment in staff and professionals.

Bond Banks
Bond banks are a creative financing option and have grown in popularity over the past several years. Roughly a dozen states now have bond banks in place. Bond banks are state-sponsored issuers that provide access to municipal markets for local infrastructure projects. Bond banks issue their own debt securities, often supported by a state credit enhancement. Some bond bank programs involve the purchase of local municipal bonds for inclusion within a pool, and the sale of bonds by the bond bank secured by the pool of local municipal bonds. Other bond bank programs work in a re-lending fashion through start-up capital used for issuances that generate proceeds that are then again used to fund projects. Successful bond banks are able to do multiple issuances and relending cycles before requiring funding for recapitalization. This ability allows bond banks to use their limited direct funding to leverage bond financing authority for larger volume. Small local communities that are unable to issue bonds due to their limited size can use a bond bank's pooled issuance program to achieve project financing.

Taxable Bond Financing
Taxable bond financing works much like tax-exempt bond financing, but lacks federal tax-exemption benefits and federal tax credit benefits. Despite the lack of federal tax-exemption, these bonds remain attractive options because many are exempt from state income taxes. Many finance agencies use taxable bonds, called "taxable tails", to complete projects that do not generate enough tax-exempt financing capacity. Taxable tails are often used as a gap-financing source to complete projects requiring additional financing support.

Important Bond Players

The bond finance process is complex, and it requires considerable oversight. In each transaction, there are a variety of players critical to ensuring that the process is effective, efficient and conducted within the scope of the law. Almost all bonds that are issued by state and local political subdivisions are accompanied by the approving legal opinion of a recognized bond counsel law firm. The bond counsel's approving legal opinion gives investors assurance as to the validity and security of the bonds, and the tax-exempt status of the interest on the bonds. Bond counsel generally represents the issuer. The underwriter's counsel is responsible for preparing various documents on behalf of the underwriter relating to the purchase and sale of the bonds such as any offering disclosure documents.

Each transaction also involves a trustee. The trustee is responsible for acting as the fiduciary agent for the bondholders. The trustee participates heavily in the disbursement of bond proceeds to fund the capital costs of the project, the payment of principal and interest to bondholders, and the coordinating of bondholder action in the event of document waivers or amendments, and bond defaults.

Other players in the process may include various counsel to the issuer, the private borrower and the trustee, as well as financial advisors to the issuer and the borrower. Coordination among and between the appropriate players throughout the process is critical to a project's success.

Bond Ratings

Bond ratings are determinations by nationally recognized rating agencies such as Standard & Poor's, Moody's and Fitch as to an issuer's credit strength in a particular financing. The rating in effect speaks to the probability that bond investors will be paid in full and on time by the borrower. Bond ratings play a very important role in the issuance process because they determine the levels and interest rates at which bonds may be issued. Bond rating agencies generally review various factors in determining an issuer's bond rating, including debt service coverage, economic factors, administrative/governmental factors and fiscal/financial performance factors.

Although bonds do not legally require a rating, market circumstances compel most issuers to have their large debt issues rated. Investors use the bond ratings to analyze the degree of risk that is associated with purchasing various public securities. High ratings reflect a low risk of non-payment on principal and interest by the issuer, whereas low ratings reflect a higher risk of non-payment.

The higher the bond rating, the lower the interest rate will be for the bonds, corresponding to the decreasing likelihood of default. All long-term bonds rated below the fourth category are judged below investment grade (speculative grade), and they are often referred to as "junk" bonds.

Wrapping Up Bedrock Tools

In each of these categories of qualified PABs, bonds must meet the specific requirements of the IRC. These tests can be complex, and they require a clear understanding before bonds may be issued in order to ensure tax-exempt status. There are also dozens of procedural and statutory requirements that go into issuing these bonds. Most of these activities are handled directly by the professionals involved in the process, but they are ultimately initiated at the issuer's request. Finance agencies should employ a comprehensive approach to understanding the bond issuance process, and they should work to educate elected leaders and board members on the potential risks and rewards involved.

In relation to economic development efforts, the bonds outlined in this chapter represent the most concrete, readily available source of public finance. Private Activity Bond use has increased exponentially over the past two decades, and today, they serve as the primary source for financing many types of projects, including infrastructure, industrial development and urban development.

This chapter provides only a brief overview of bond finance. For more information on bond finance, refer to CDFA's Industry Primer: Development Bond Finance Reference Guide and/or Advanced Bond Finance Reference Guide.

CHAPTER 4

TARGETED TOOLS

Understanding Targeted Financing Tools

Direct and targeted financing tools are the fastest growing area of development finance. Targeted financing tools differ from other tools because they target specific geographic areas in a community, offering incentives, tax rebates, credits and unique financing structures that drive investment and development within that geographic footprint. Most of these targeted tools fall into a category called special district financing, and they all provide a slightly different approach to a similar concept. This guide will highlight several popular tools used throughout the country.

The goal of targeted and special assessment district financing tools is to catalyze investment and transform the actual or perceived real estate values of a given geographic area. These programs are also designed to set aside financial resources for investment, maintenance, beautification, safety and other improvements to the built environment. Many communities use the resources derived from special assessment district financing programs to develop and market business districts, cultural centers and other attractions.

Targeted and special assessment district financing tools have been widely successful, yet they are still under-utilized throughout the country. Tax increment finance – the leading targeted financing tool employed today – is an exception to the rule. Communities employing these tools have shown sizeable increases in property values and overall business development and community improvement. Large market cities such as Baltimore, Washington, D.C., Los Angeles, Atlanta, Chicago and even smaller communities such as Boise, Des Moines, Louisville, Columbus and others have applied these tools effectively.

Types of Targeted Tools

Targeted and special assessment district financing tools typically fall into two categories. The first category of tools is designed to generate new taxes in a geographic area through improvements to the built environment. These improvements increase property, sales or other taxes, which can in turn be used to finance some of the improvements. The second category of tools allows business and industry to generate funds through tax assessments. These assessments, often self-imposed, in turn finance improvements in the geographic area. The following represents a summary of available tools.

Tax Increment Financing (TIF)

Tax increment financing (TIF) is referred to in a variety of ways throughout the country. These terms include tax allocation district (TAD – Georgia), tax increment reinvestment zone (TIRZ – Texas), community reinvestment area (CRA – Florida) and revenue allocation district (RAD – New Jersey). Generally, however, TIFs adhere to a similar structure and function in a similar fashion, regardless of geography. Today, 49 states and the District of Columbia employ TIF tools, with rules and regulations varying by state. It is recommended that finance professionals, community leaders and economic development professionals consult their relevant state statutes before attempting to employ a TIF program. The use of legal professionals and expert consultants is also recommended to ensure the use of best practices.

A TIF district is a mechanism for capturing the future tax benefits of real estate improvements, in order to pay for the present cost of those improvements. It can be used to channel funding toward improvements in distressed or underdeveloped areas where development would not otherwise occur.

On the surface, the TIF process is relatively straightforward. Typically, the first step is to set the TIF district's geographic boundaries. The second step is to establish the initial assessed value of the land in the district. Furthermore, an analysis of current tax revenue from property tax, sales tax and other taxes should be conducted to benchmark the current tax level. A TIF district generates money for development or redevelopment for a local government by capturing the tax revenue – or increment – above the initial assessed value during the life of the district. The tax increment from a TIF district is created without raising taxes, and also without dipping into the base tax revenues present at the time of adoption. The increment thus becomes a repayment stream for debt used to finance some aspects of what is driving the increase – such as retail, commercial, residential or mixed-use development.

Tax increment finance is a popular development finance tool generally used to address blight, promote neighborhood stability and inspire district-oriented development. While each state's TIF statute is different, common policy goals and objectives exist. These intentions include blight elimination, something discussed in nearly every state's statute, and infrastructure additions and improvements.

A TIF district is often used to advance economic development priorities, including:

- Guiding public finance dollars towards targeted investment and development
- Developing industry niches and opening new markets for services that do not exist in a given geographic area
- Supporting overall development within a specific geographic area
- Reusing existing infrastructure and cleaning up polluted or brownfield land
- Creating or retaining jobs and supporting industrial development

A TIF district is a powerful tool that can address many needs in a community. It is often used to encourage development, eliminate blight, address environmental issues, and facilitate adaptive reuse.

Tax increment finance uses the increased property and/or sales taxes generated by a new development to finance costs related to that particular development. These costs may include: public infrastructure, land acquisition, relocation, demolition, utilities, debt service and planning costs. A TIF district may also be used for a variety of other improvements, including:

- Sewer expansion and repair
- Storm drainage
- Street construction & expansion
- Water supply
- Park improvements
- Bridge construction & repair
- Curb & sidewalk work
- Traffic control
- Street lighting
- Landscaping
- Property acquisition
- Building acquisition
- Demolition & clearance work
- Parking structures
- Environmental remediation

Individual states authorize local government units to designate tax increment financing districts. Either city or county development entities or nonprofit redevelopment entities typically administer this type of financing. A city council or a private board or commission typically governs the local agency.

A TIF district, or the area capturing the tax increment itself, is drawn in order to direct benefits to a designated area – typically an area that is economically sluggish or physically distressed. The life of a district can be anywhere from 10-40 years, or enough time to pay back pay back the costs or bonds issued to fund the improvements.

In essence, tax increment financing has provided local governments with a funding mechanism that does not rely on federal funds, that escapes state limits on revenue and expenditures, and that does not apply any new tax on municipal taxpayers. Today, there are thousands of TIF districts in place, making improvements in local communities across the country.

This section provides only a brief overview of TIF. For more information on TIF, refer to CDFA's Tax Increment Finance Best Practices Reference Guide.

Special Assessment District Financing

Special assessment district financing mechanisms are also a common but under-utilized tool. Nearly every state provides some form of special assessment district financing. Most states offer more than one option. These tools are known by a variety of names and can be structured in a variety of ways, but there are two predominant methods. The first method is the assembly of business and neighborhood groups into a district to generate funding for projects and programs. The second approach is a directly targeted assessment program organized by local government. In the business/neighborhood focused model, a local nonprofit or development agency manages the district, while in the government focused model, the local government manages it. The following is an overview of both approaches.

Business and Neighborhood Districts

Business and neighborhood-focused districts are typically run by property owners in the district. These owners impose self-assessed taxes on themselves in order to generate funds for physical improvements or other amenities. Some examples of these programs include:

- Business Improvement District (BID)
- Special Improvement District (SID)
- Community Improvement District (CID)
- Neighborhood Improvement District (NID)

Services and programs may include security and safety patrols, economic development, graffiti removal, snow removal, marketing, beautification projects and cleanliness programs. In states where these programs are permitted, local government performs the task of establishing the district in cooperation with the district's property owners.

Once the district is authorized, the assessed tax is paid to the government through a collection process. Once collected, the government returns the special assessment to the district's management entity, typically a nonprofit or redevelopment agency, and the funds are then used to finance improvements.

Such districts have been known to finance revolving loan funds and other lending programs to assist businesses to effect physical improvements to their buildings and storefronts and general business growth. These types of business districts are particularly popular in communities where basic services do not provide adequate attention to business or neighborhood needs. This tool allows the private sector to partner with government to focus on strengths and opportunities that exist in business districts. In addition, these tools allow the private sector to direct taxes toward their own investments, thus making government more effective and keeping business districts prosperous.

Government Districts

Government focused districts come in many shapes and sizes. These districts often provide services that are similar in scope to those provided by business districts. However, in these cases, government entities typically direct the work of these districts. Examples of government-driven districts include:

- Special Services District (SSD)
- Special Assessment District (SAD)
- Community Facilities District (CFD)
- Community Development District (CDD)
- Transportation Improvement District (TID)

This approach can be effective in directing government resources, through a property owner's self-imposed assessment, toward the maintenance or redevelopment of designated districts.

Such government directed programs have largely focused on infrastructure development, such as transportation, roads, sewers and community amenities like schools and public facilities. These districts are typically formed in undeveloped or underdeveloped areas where commercial and residential development cannot otherwise be supported. Government focused districts also allow for a wider array of financing options. The use of bonds is one tool used to finance these projects.

Some of these districts can be used in conjunction with other tools (i.e., TIF and revolving loan funds) to assess an additional tax on property in a redevelopment area. This extra assessment can be used to finance added services or amenities in the district and to pay debt service on the bonds used to finance the project. Special assessment districts have also been used to establish road and sewer revolving loan funds, and these infrastructure improvements help to encourage economic development.

Finally, government directed districts offer the ability for governmental jurisdictions to work together on projects by creating joint assessment districts. In communities where overlapping or continuous governmental jurisdictions are developing, assessment tools can be used to bring varying entities together. Cooperative joint assessment agreements can provide for shared services, investment and amenity provisions. The ability for varying units of government to cooperate on projects, service delivery and economic development is a major benefit of special assessment district financing.

Targeting Specific Projects –
Brownfields & Sustainable Development

While geographically targeted financing tools have been the focus of this chapter, another targeted financing concept also exists. This concept is based on specific types of development, namely brownfields and sustainable development.

Brownfields development is an ever-growing field, due to the prevalence of under-utilized land in urban and industrial areas. Many resources at the local, state and federal level address brownfields acquisition, remediation and redevelopment.

Nearly all of the tools in the development finance toolbox may be used to address these opportunities as well.

Tools for financing brownfields redevelopment include:

- Tax increment finance – qualified public improvements after remediation, as well as acquisition and remediation, depending upon the state statute
- Tax credits – state and local tax credits for remediation and redevelopment
- Loan funds – state and local loan funds for acquisition, remediation and also, potentially, redevelopment
- Grants – state and local grants for remediation

Green development is a relatively new discipline in economic development finance. Most of the nation's renewable energy efforts are lumped into green development through the New Clean Renewable Energy Bonds (New CREBs) and Qualified Energy Conservation Bonds (QECBs), which are discussed in Chapter 3. There have also been a few pilot green bond programs conducted at the federal level.

Currently, green development is driven by many of the same financing tools as more typical development, such as TIF, tax credits and loan funds. Some states have begun to award incentives, and also lower loan interest rates for green and sustainable development. The municipal bond industry is beginning to recognize the strength of green/sustainable projects through robust support of issuances supporting these concepts. In addition, the private venture and innovation capital industry has been the quickest to take the lead in supporting green development through clean-tech financing and other seed fund investment in green technologies.

Tool Distinctions

Targeted and special assessment district financing tools can be very complex, and require considerable dedication to program management, legal understanding and due diligence. In the financing toolbox, these particular tools are most beneficial when focusing on a specific geographic area, because they are flexible and can be used in conjunction with other tools such as bonds, tax credits and revolving loan funds.

Every state has different rules and regulations for the use of targeted and special assessment district financing tools. Not all states employ the same tools, and what works in Ohio may be vastly different from what works in Arizona. Moreover, tools of a very similar nature are often referred to by varying names, making it difficult to draw conclusions from different regions of the country.

Wrapping Up Targeted Financing Tools

Targeted financing tools are the most effective for investing precious public resources into economic development. Using the powers provided by state law and the financing capacity of governmental entities, these tools can foster redevelopment. Such approaches should always be used in a comprehensive manner consistent with the community's overall economic development strategy, and they should also be used in concert with other tools in the development finance toolbox. Perhaps most importantly, targeted financing tools should be used thoughtfully and creatively to address community needs, while they strengthen and diversify a geographic area's economic base.

Understanding Investment Tools

Unique financing solutions provide incentives for individuals and companies to invest in new machinery, technology and construction. These resources – tax credits, seed and venture capital and angel funds being the most abundant among them – are key elements of the development finance toolbox. While each program is different, they have a shared outcome – catalyzing investment.

Individual states have also created tax credit programs and state-sponsored seed and venture capital programs that fit in the investment tools category. Some states have also created programs that provide tax credits for the creation of venture capital funds. Such funds benefit private investors as well as businesses and entrepreneurs. These programs can be a win-win for taxpayers and entrepreneurs who are developing new industries in a community.

The federal government has also created programs to help catalyze investment. Federal tax credit programs provide a powerful tool for economic development professionals. These programs help to catalyze a range of investments, including historic rehabilitation, environmental remediation, affordable housing, underserved real estate markets, and renewable energy.

To take advantage of the development finance toolbox, economic development professionals must be able to understand and use investment tools, which can make a measurable difference in fostering economic development.

Tax Credit Finance

Although they are one of the most accessible tools in the development finance toolbox, tax credits, which are often complex and difficult to understand, are widely under-utilized. According to CDFA research, less than 5% of finance agencies regularly employ state and federal tax credit programs.

In order to catalyze investment on the local level using tax credits, it is critical to understand their history and impact. Tax credits have become increasingly popular, as federal resources have diminished over the past 20 years. As federal and state governments recognized the benefits of tax credits and incentives, they developed programs to address economic development needs. Over time, these programs have helped to provide a wide range of financing options for brownfields redevelopment, historic rehabilitation, low-income housing, emerging markets, venture capital, and job creation in a wide range of industries.

Tax credits can be used for several purposes in development projects: to provide an increased internal rate of return for investors, to reduce the interest rates on a particular financing package, and perhaps most importantly, to provide a repayment method for investors in place of cash. In the latter case, the credits can often be sold on the secondary market to generate income.

Tax credits are also flexible. They can be used in urban, rural and suburban communities, and in some cases on a regional basis. They can also provide a targeted impact by addressing many different community sectors, such as low-income neighborhoods, historic districts and underserved markets that present opportunities for new investment.

Tax credit programs bring many different stakeholders to the table, thus leveraging their impact. Tax credits may attract investors, businesses, government entities, nonprofits, community development organizations, industrial development authorities, economic development corporations, financial institutions, pension funds, universities, foundations, state governments, and the federal government.

Perhaps most importantly, tax credits do not disappear during economic downturns, unlike many other financing programs. On the contrary, tax credit programs are often both dependable and politically popular.

How Tax Credits Work

Tax credit programs allow businesses and investors to claim a tax credit for committing resources to a project or business. Such a resource commitment could be an investment in a bricks and mortar real estate project or a cash investment in a business. The distributor of the tax credit is authorized to issue credit based on the actual outlay of resources as evidenced by the investor.

Tax credit programs also help to encourage private sector leveraging of resources, and act as a catalyst for public/private partnerships. Tax credits also create "secondary financial markets" for the sellers and buyers of the credits.

Tax Credit Distinctions

Tax credits have been slow to grow in popularity for a number of reasons, most notably, the existence of easier financing such as loans, grants and bonds. Tax credits are complex, the application process is lengthy, and once a deal is in place, a great deal of documentation and scrutiny is required. As a result of this complexity, private investors are often unwilling to engage in these programs.

The tax credit application process brings with it a considerable amount of scrutiny. The investors must prove that "but for" the provision of these tax credits, the targeted project would not attract the necessary private investment.

Tax credits are performance-based financing tools, and once implemented, their worth must be proven. Such data collection, as well as the verification of investment goals, requires a great deal of due diligence.

Misconceptions about tax credit programs abound. In the media and in public perception, tax credit deals are often lumped together with tax incentives and tax abatements. However, unlike tax incentives and abatements, the tax credit user must demonstrate the outlay of resources in order to receive the benefits.

Finally, tax credit programs are often marketed ineffectively. The federal government does little to market available tax credit programs. States often provide a wide variety of programs, making it difficult to market programs effectively and difficult for potential users to distinguish among them.

Types of Programs

Tax credit programs cover dozens of industry and business types and vary between states. This section will cover the four main federal tax credit programs as well as a few smaller federal programs available to communities.

Historic Preservation Tax Incentives

Rehabilitation tax credits were established to discourage unnecessary demolition of older buildings, and also to slow capital flight from older urban areas. This type of incentive offers a credit against the total federal taxes owed, and is taken for the year in which the renovated building is "put into service" or completed. The credit is equal to 20% of qualified rehabilitation expenditures devoted to a certified historic structure, and 10% of qualified rehabilitation expenditures devoted to a building not considered a certified historic structure. Historic preservation tax credits have often been used to complement brownfield redevelopment. Property tax abatement and low interest loans are the most commonly paired incentives to this federal tax credit.

Historic rehabilitation tax credits are both popular and widely used. In recent years, states such as Virginia and Ohio have created state programs that complement this federal program. These state programs, typically used in conjunction with the federal historic tax credits on a given project, provide additional public assistance for projects that need support.

Sources: National Parks Service, www.nps.gov/hps/tps/tax/index.htm, 2009 Historic Tax Credits, Presentation by Bill MacRostie, MacRostie Historic Advisors LLC, January 2008

Federal Brownfield Tax Incentive

The Brownfields Tax Incentive helps to reduce an investor's tax burden by lowering the investor's taxable income. The incentive allows the investor to claim the eligible costs of cleaning up brownfields land as current expenses – rather than capitalizing these expenses as long-term assets. Many investors prefer such deductions, because they reduce their current income and allow them to capture the tax savings right away, not down the road. The Brownfields Tax Incentive, which provides an immediate incentive to offset short-term cleanup costs, encourages cleanup and redevelopment of polluted land.

Source: U.S. Environmental Protection Agency, Brownfield and Land Revitalization, www.epa.gov/brownfields/bftaxinc.htm, 2009

New Markets Tax Credits

The New Markets Tax Credit (NMTC) was created to generate additional capital for economic development projects in low-income communities. The NMTC provides a 39% federal tax credit for Qualified Equity Investments (QEIs) made through investment in Community Development Entities (CDEs) working in targeted low-income communities.

The New Markets Tax Credit is taken over a seven-year period. A 5% annual credit is taken for the first three years, followed by a 6% credit over the last four years, for a total of thirty-nine percent of the initial investment. NMTCs help borrowers and projects achieve lower interest rates and potential equity stakes at the end of the credit period, which enhances the project and incentivizes more investment.

For the purpose of the NMTC program, low-income communities are considered to be census tracts with a poverty rate of at least 20%, or census tracts in which median family income is below 80% of the area median family income.

NMTC investments may include loans to businesses, to commercial, industrial and/or retail developments, and to developing for-sale housing. NMTC investments must take place in qualified areas, yet a wide array of communities fit in these guidelines, making this type of credit an essential tool.

Source: U.S. Department of Treasury, CDFI Fund, www.cdfifund.gov, 2009

Low-Income Housing Tax Credits

The federal government created the Low Income Housing Tax Credit (LIHTC) in 1986 to promote the construction and rehabilitation of housing for low-income individuals. This tax credit provides a means by which developers, corporations or individuals may raise capital for the construction, acquisition and rehabilitation of housing for low-income individuals.

Each year, states receive an inflation-adjusted, per person funding allocation for the issuance of tax credits for qualified housing development projects. These tax credits are typically used to leverage private capital, which in turn makes possible the construction, acquisition and rehabilitation of affordable housing.

State housing authorities are responsible for administering these programs and also for working with local communities to distribute the allocations. The credit ranges from 4 to 9% percent, depending on the level of federal subsidies provided to the project. The tax credit is taken over a ten year period, and requires a fifteen year compliance period.

Source: Low-Income Housing Tax Credit Basics, Presentation by Brad Weinberg, Novogradac & Company, November 2006

Empowerment Zones (EZ) & Renewal Communities (RC)

A number of tax credits are available through targeted economic development programs initiated by the federal government. Empowerment Zones (EZs) offer approximately $5.3 billion in incentives for small and large businesses, including an employment credit that allows businesses to take an annual tax credit of up to $3,000 for each employee who lives and works in the designated geographic area. EZs also provide worker opportunity credits that allow businesses to take a tax credit of up to $2,400 for each new employee between the ages of eighteen and thirty-nine who lives in the EZ.

Federally designated Renewal Communities (RCs) offer an estimated $5.6 billion in incentives. Businesses may claim an annual tax credit of up to $1,500 for each employee who lives and works for a business in the RC. Businesses may also claim a worker opportunity credit of up to $2,400 for each new employee between the ages of eighteen and thirty-nine who lives in the RC.

Source: U.S. Department of Housing & Urban Development, Community Renewal Initiative, www.hud.gov, 2009

Energy Production Credits

This program provides a per kilowatt-hour federally adjusted tax credit for a variety of energy producing activities including wind, biomass, hydro, geothermal and other renewable energy sources.

Energy Investment Tax Credit

Tax credits are available for qualified solar investment for both commercial and residential properties.

State Tax Credits

Every state and the District of Columbia offer state tax credit programs. These programs address a number of different investment areas, including:

- Venture capital investment
- Low-income housing
- Job creation
- Machinery and equipment
- Targeted area redevelopment
- Brownfield cleanup
- Wage adjustment credits
- Industry specific credits

State tax credit programs have grown significantly over the past ten years, and innovative and targeted programs are spread throughout the country.

Innovation Finance –
Seed & Venture Capital and Angel Funds

The second most commonly used investment tool is innovation finance. This tool focuses on growing economic innovation through development of new technology, new businesses and industries, and entrepreneurial activity. Innovation finance includes seed and venture capital and angel funds.

The innovation finance industry is largely managed by the private sector. Investment companies and individual investors collaborate in order to bring available capital into the market and to finance projects.

Seed & Venture Capital

Seed capital is an initial investment into a new business venture or product line. Often, this investment allows an entrepreneur to launch a new venture without drawing upon traditional lending sources (such as bank financing). As a general rule, seed capital is provided by private investors in exchange for a high rate of return (ranging from fifteen to thirty percent) on their investment.

Seed capital recipients are typically businesses or entrepreneurs with less than one year of history. In most cases, they have not yet produced a commercial product or service. Often, these young companies are unable to obtain funding from traditional sources, such as banks, and must turn to capital from investors in order to grow. In turn, these investors often seek an equity or ownership position in the new company. This represents a considerable tradeoff, as the entrepreneur must cede an ownership interest or pay an unusually high rate of return in order to gain access to capital.

Venture capital, also known as private equity, is another form of financing, and it is more commonplace than seed financing. Venture capitalists are financiers that take a role in the management of young, growing companies. Venture capital firms, the entities that provide such financing, are generally private partnerships or corporations funded by private and public pension funds, endowment funds, foundations, corporations, individuals and foreign investors. Venture capital is different from seed capital because venture capital firms typically do not invest in companies until they are somewhat established, whereas seed capital may be used to develop a business idea into a company.

Venture capitalists often play a hands-on role in the management of a new, growing company, and may also assist with product development. They typically take a high risk in anticipation of a relatively higher rate of return over a period of time (typically five to seven years). In recent decades, venture capitalists have nurtured the growth of technology firms and other industries, resulting in job creation, economic growth and greater international competitiveness. Currently, over fifty percent of venture capital investments come from institutional pension funds, both public and private. The balance comes from endowments, foundations, insurance companies, banks, individuals and other entities that are seeking to diversify their portfolios with this class of investments.

Venture capital firms typically invest in young companies, often before a product has been developed. These firms may also invest in companies at various stages of the business life cycle. For instance, they may provide capital to companies in their first or second stage of development. This is known as "early stage investing." Venture capital firms may also provide financing to help companies grow beyond their current capacity. This is called "expansion stage financing."

Some venture capital firms focus on later stage investing, because such an investment may help companies leverage or attract additional public financing, which in turn may help the company increase its return.

While venture capitalists are known for investing in technology companies, they also invest in more traditional businesses such as construction, industrial products and business services. Some firms specialize in retail company investment. Others focus on investing in "socially responsible" companies.

There are several types of venture capital firms, but most invest their capital through funds. Venture capital firms may be affiliates or subsidiaries of a commercial or investment bank or insurance company and make investments on behalf of outside investors. Others are subsidiaries of non-financial, industrial corporations and make investments on behalf of the parent company.

Other organizations include government-affiliated investment programs that help start-up companies. One such vehicle is the Small Business Investment Company (SBIC) program administered by the Small Business Administration. Using this program, a venture capital firm may augment its own funds with federal money and leverage its investment in qualified companies.

Like a mutual fund company, a venture capital firm may have more than one fund in existence at any given time. A venture capital firm may close one fund after the initial investment is repaid, and then establish another fund so that it may continue to attract investors and make investments. It is not uncommon for a successful firm to raise six or seven funds over the span of ten to fifteen years. The investment strategy of these various funds may be similar or dissimilar. A firm might have one fund with a specific investment focus (such as minority-led businesses) and another with no specific focus, and a diverse portfolio.

Seed and venture capital programs exist throughout the country. While the public sector may help to initiate such programs, they are largely operated by the private sector. Economic development practitioners can help to foster economic activity by steering new companies, entrepreneurs and start-ups towards venture capital and private equity firms in their states or communities. This type of funding is critical in providing capital for emerging businesses.

Source: National Venture Capital Association, www.nvca.org, 2008

Angel Investment

Angel investors offer the largest private source of capital for early-stage companies. Venture capital is typically aimed at more fully developed companies requiring investments of five million dollars or more. Angel investors, on the other hand, provide private financing for emerging companies that are too small to attract venture capital, but too big to rely on family or friends. Typically, the amount of the investment ranges from $50,000 to $1 million or more. Angel investments can be used at critical points in a company's development, enabling it to get past funding hurdles in its early years. Angel investors also provide hands-on technical assistance to the companies they invest in.

Angel investors are wealthy individuals with a high income or net worth that allows them to make substantial investments in these new companies. Currently, it is estimated that there are as many as 350,000 angel investors in the U.S. While such investors have previously focused on urban metropolitan areas, this has shifted in recent years, as they have begun to invest in companies in rural areas.

According to the Angel Capital Education Foundation, angel investors provide about ninety percent of outside equity capital for start-ups. The Foundation also states that angel investors provide more funding to more companies than venture capital firms, and that they have a better track record with companies going public.

However, angel investors seeking to invest in companies may find the prospect daunting. Reading business plans and sourcing deals can be time-consuming. Due diligence on such investments may require the assistance of outside experts or legal support, both of which can be expensive. Once an investment is made, monitoring that investment and determining follow-on or exit strategies may also be time consuming. One way to overcome these obstacles is to join a group of angel investors. With such an arrangement, members typically share the work, expertise, risks and rewards of investing.

Angel groups exist at both the state and local levels throughout the country. National organizations such as the Angel Capital Association are working to expand the profile of this important economic development tool. Economic development professionals can help support start-up companies by connecting them with individual angel investors as well as angel investor groups. Because angel investment represents a significant portion of the early stage financing that is available in the United States, understanding how it is used and the ability to access it are critically important to building the development finance toolbox.

Source: Steve Mercil, RAIN Source Capital, Organizing Angel Investment to Benefit Angels, Companies, and Communities, Community Development Investment News, Federal Reserve of San Francisco, Volume 2 Issue 3, 2006

Community Development Venture Capital

Community development venture capital (CDVC) funds use the tools of venture capital in order to encourage entrepreneurial growth and job creation in distressed communities. CDVC funds use a "double bottom line" approach; that is, they pursue both social and financial returns on their investments. Currently, there are approximately sixty CDVC funds across the United States.

Much like venture capital firms, CDVC funds make equity, near-equity, and debt investments in for-profit businesses with rapid growth potential. CDVC funds also seek an ownership position in these companies in return for such an investment. Many community development corporations lend flexible equity capital to small businesses in areas where these resources are limited.

While CDVC funds vary in size, research shows that they have an average capitalization of approximately $13.1 million. Not-for-profit funds typically fall into one of two categories: having less than $1 million, or more than $5 million available for CDVC investments. Banks are the largest single supplier of capital for such funds, followed by corporations and foundations. Federal, state and local governments, as well as public pension funds, may also provide capital for these funds.

In recent years, private firms have also started CDVC funds. These firms typically employ management teams with private equity experience, and connections to local financial leaders such as bankers, corporations and economic development agencies. These funds are typically structured like venture capital funds to ensure confidence and familiarity with investors. This structure also helps to ensure that the fund's focus is on the social mission, not operations, thus accelerating the funds growth and investment appetite.

In recent years, CDVC funds have become popular across the U.S. as a way to encourage socially responsible investing. Economic development professionals and leaders should consider developing these programs in order to enhance access to capital and foster entrepreneurial activity in areas under-served by traditional economic development finance tools.

Source: Brian T. Schmitt, Community Development Venture Capital Alliance, www.cdvca. org, 2008

Venture Capital Tax Credit Programs

In recent years, a number of state venture capital tax credit programs have been developed to invest in rapidly growing businesses with governmental support. Through these programs, states target formal venture funds, or in some cases, individual investors who are looking for business investment opportunities. Models of this program can vary from state to state, but generally have elements consistent with the provision of tax credits for the investment in venture capital funds. This concept encourages indirect investment into venture capital funds rather than actual companies. The funds in turn invest in a desired portfolio of businesses and return profits to the investors. In return for this investment, the states provide tax credits to the investor. There are also variations that allow for fund raising through the provision of contingent tax credits for qualified investment.

Source: The Sandler Report, The Effective Use of Tax Credits in State Venture Capital Programs, Daniel Sandler, Faculty of Law, The University of Western Ontario, 2004

National Science Foundation (NSF) – SBIR & STTR Programs
The National Science Foundation (NSF) is an independent federal agency created by Congress to promote the progress of science, health and national defense. NSF is the funding source for approximately 20 percent of all federally supported basic research conducted by U.S. colleges and universities. In many fields such as mathematics, computer science and the social sciences, NSF is the major source of federal backing. NSF runs the successful Small Business Innovation Research (SBIR) and Small Business Technology Transfer (STTR) programs. Eleven federal departments participate in the SBIR program; five departments participate in the STTR program awarding billions in funding to small high-tech businesses. Both programs provided competitive grants for small business development for high-tech and innovation industry business development.

The NSF website provides detailed program information at www.nsf.gov.

Incubators

Business incubation programs are another important investment tool. These programs can provide targeted resources to help grow start-up companies. A business incubator may be set up as a physical site, with onsite management and services, or it may be set up virtually, with a network of contacts and support professionals.

The goal of business incubators is to help companies gain financial stability and self-sufficiency. Incubator graduates create jobs, revitalize neighborhoods and commercialize new technologies.

Successful incubators provide management guidance and technical assistance. A physical incubator site may provide services that assist a company's growth, including affordable rental space, flexible lease terms, shared services, and equipment and tech support. Some incubators also provide resources that allow companies to gain access to capital for later stage development.

Incubators vary considerably in how they are structured, how they deliver services, and the type of companies they serve. Incubators also help to address a wide variety of goals, including rural development, employment growth, technology development, and wealth creation in distressed neighborhoods.

Traditional business incubators have largely focused on technology companies. However, in recent years, new incubators have emerged targeting such industries as food processing, medical technology, space and ceramics technology, arts and crafts, and software development. Incubators have also created programs to support micro-enterprise creation, woman and minority-led business, sustainable/green business, and telecommunications firms.

Business incubators foster economic development in communities and regions by developing strong public-private partnerships and supporting businesses, and they are a critical tool in the development finance toolbox.

Source: National Business Incubation Association, www.nbia.org, 2008

Wrapping Up Investment Tools

Investment tools are the most complex tools in the development finance toolbox, and also the most under-utilized. Investment tools appear complex and difficult to administer to many economic development professionals, yet they are critical tools and should not be ignored.

Tax credits help to support projects while providing benefits to a wide range of investors, developers, banks and other key players. Seed, venture and angel capital investments provide the majority of private financing to new and growing businesses across the U.S.

Putting such programs to work in a community takes time, patience, and a dedication to program development. However, once established, these investment tools will prove critical in fostering economic development.

ACCESS TO CAPITAL LENDING TOOLS

Understanding Access to Capital Tools

Capital tools, the fourth area of the development finance toolbox, include revolving loan funds, mezzanine finance, loan guarantees and micro-enterprise financing. These tools, while important, are widely under-utilized.

Small businesses are the economic lifeblood of our communities – they make up 99.7%of all firms, employ half of all private sector employees and 45% of total U.S. private payroll, and have generated 60 to 80% of all new jobs annually over the past decade. Yet for decades, economic development professionals have neglected small businesses, focusing instead on large-scale clients such as manufacturing companies and multi-tenant office users.

Economic development professionals should understand the tools available to help small businesses access capital. Fostering small business growth will pay dividends down the road because it will lead to increased investment, real estate improvements, job creation and tax growth.

Source: U.S. Small Business Administration, www.sba.gov, 2007

What is Access to Capital?

Small businesses need access to affordable, reliable capital to get started, for their day to day operations, and for new investments. They need capital simply to get through the day, as "working capital" allows small businesses to pay their bills while investing in future growth.

Capital programs vary widely. Some communities fund a range of types of business development through a revolving loan fund; others focus their efforts on minority or women-owned businesses as a mechanism to spur growth.

Communities that offer financing are able to build relationships with the business community, to act as a partner and investor in the small businesses they support, and to develop strong commercial districts.

Types of Capital Access Programs

Capital programs are a key facet of the development finance toolbox. They can be tailored to address small financing needs as well as large scale projects. This category represents the largest, most flexible part of the toolbox.

Capital programs range from large loan funds supported by the federal government to small, linked deposit programs supported by local governments and banking institutions. This range of programs shows that federal, state and local governments often play a key role in providing access to capital.

In the Investment Tools chapter of this guide, we discussed funding for start-up and entrepreneurial businesses. In this chapter, we will discuss tools that can be used to provide capital to established businesses, including both broad and tailored programs, such as those providing funding to minority-owned businesses.

Revolving Loan Funds

Revolving loan funds (RLFs) are finance tools that can be used to help grow small and mid-sized businesses. A RLF is a funding pool that replenishes itself. As existing loan holders make payments, the payments are recycled to fund new loans. While the majority of RLFs support local businesses, some target specific areas such as health care, minority or women business development, and environmental remediation.

Revolving loan funds provide businesses with a flexible source of capital that can be combined with conventional sources. RLF funds can be used to fill the gap between the loan amount a borrower obtains from a private lender and the amount needed to sustain a business.

Revolving loan funds issue loans at competitive rates, making them attractive to borrowers. Yet many studies show that borrowers often find access to capital, as well as flexibility in collateral and terms, to be more important than favorable interest rates.

Because RLFs must replenish the fund to make future loans, such programs must maintain a balance between charging attractive rates and earning a reasonable rate of return.

RLF loan funds are typically used for operating capital, acquisition of land and buildings, new construction, facade and building renovation, landscape and property improvements, and machinery and equipment. Loan duration varies according to use of the funds. For instance, a loan for working capital may have a term of three to five years, loans for equipment may have terms of up to ten years, and real estate loans may have terms of fifteen to twenty years.

RLF loan amounts vary widely, and some may be quite small (under $10,000). Larger amounts ($100,000 to $250,000 and up) are typically available when a borrower has already secured a commitment from private lenders.

To establish a revolving loan fund, the capital usually comes from a mix of public sources (local, state, and federal governments) and private sources (financial and philanthropic institutions). This funding is usually a grant and does not need to be paid back.

Most revolving loan funds are at least partially funded by local, public sources of capital. If a RLF is exclusively funded by local sources, it may have greater flexibility, as state and federal funding often come with restrictions.

To fund a RLF, state and local governments use a combination of tax set-asides, general obligation bonds, funds appropriations from state legislatures, annual dues from counties or municipalities, and state lottery funds. The federal government is another common source of this capital.

Though revolving loan funds provide capital to projects with above-average risk, borrowers must nevertheless go through a loan underwriting process. For a loan to be issued, businesses must provide detailed financial information and demonstrate that the project is likely to succeed. Projects must contribute to economic growth and community revitalization. Borrowers must meet performance measures used to assess the success of the loan fund over time.

A Loan Review Committee or board of directors is typically responsible for reviewing loan proposals, establishing an administrative body (public, nonprofit, or private), and hiring an entity to manage the fund. This committee or board typically includes professionals from a variety of sectors, including lawyers, lenders, business people, community development professionals, and local government professionals.

Revolving loan funds are staffed by financial specialists. In some cases, each team member is responsible for a different stage of the lending process. For instance, one staff person may specialize in loan packaging, while another may specialize in monitoring existing loans, an approach that is best for funds issuing a higher volume of loans. For funds that issue a low volume of loans, an alternative approach would be to assign each loan to a staff member that monitors it from beginning to end.

RLF programs carry the risk of borrower default as well as constant pressure to replenish a fund so it may continue to make loans. However, through sound policies and procedures, these issues can be easily addressed and managed throughout the life of a fund.

Mezzanine Funds

Mezzanine financing can be used to help finance small businesses that do not qualify for a loan through a traditional lending institution. Literally speaking, a mezzanine is the mid-level of a theater or auditorium; metaphorically, mezzanine funds occupy a middle tier of risk in economic development finance, less risky than equity or venture capital, but more risky than senior bank debt.

Mezzanine financing is often used for companies that have moved beyond the start-up stage, but do not have the footing to attract traditional lenders. Borrowers are required to demonstrate proven cash flow, strong management and operations, a business plan, and growth potential.

Small businesses may use mezzanine financing to provide working capital during periods of rapid growth. Often, mezzanine financing allows higher leverage or less rigid credit requirements than typical bank underwriters. Such financing may also provide a means of preserving capital or extending repayment terms.

Mezzanine funds can be allocated toward real estate loans, equipment loans, and expansion loans. These funds may also support the development of affordable housing and community facilities. The loan term and rate depends on the use of the funds; working capital and equipment costs are shorter term (from 5-7 years) while real estate loans have terms of fifteen years or more. Debt can be repaid at the end of the term and carry interest rates between 10 and 15%. Community development loans are typically in smaller amounts ($50,000 to $500,000), while loans for larger businesses could be up to several million dollars.

Sources of mezzanine financing include community development financial institutions (CDFIs), development corporations, insurance companies, mutual and pension funds, and private investors. A commonly cited advantage of mezzanine financing is that it is cheaper than equity financing and does not require the borrower to give up equity. In addition, mezzanine financing offers businesses more flexibility to meet their cash flow needs, to seek long-term commitments from other investors, and to expand into new markets.

One disadvantage of mezzanine financing is ceding independence to lender scrutiny, something that may prove unattractive to individuals who are accustomed to making business decisions without outside influence. Lenders may require a vote on the board of directors and may hold a borrower accountable if the business does not achieve growth projections. This type of financing may also restrict how a borrower can spend the money.

Mezzanine financing can be particularly helpful in the area of community development. Community-oriented financial institutions and development corporations have historically used this tool to provide loans to companies in low to moderate-income communities with limited access to financing.

Mezzanine funds in California, for example, have supported housing for public sector workers such as teachers, nurses and firefighters. The state government is working on programs designed to address the urban housing shortage and housing costs. The state of Texas provides another example. Mezzanine funds in Texas are helping to facilitate the development and expansion of minority-owned small businesses.

Loan Guarantees

Loan guarantees allow risk to be shifted from a private lending institution to a third party participant – usually a government entity. This guarantee reduces private lender risk, which encourages the private lenders to make loans and also makes capital for small businesses more available. The third party guarantor must be willing and able to repay the borrower's obligations to the lending institution in the event of default or loss.

There are many varieties of guarantee programs, and each has different rules, regulations and characteristics. In some cases, a percentage of the loan is guaranteed through phases of the project, and aspects of the guarantee expire as the loan matures. In some instances, such as financing in distressed communities, the guarantee is only necessary during the start up phase. As the project and the community undergo development, lending risks are relieved, and the guarantees become less crucial. Eventually, lending in the community is no longer considered risky, and capital becomes more readily available.

Loan guarantees are a win-win for government and lending institutions if the projects are successful, and both parties achieve a return on their investment. Communities that employ guarantee programs usually partner with established lending institutions with a history of supporting economic development. At the state and local level, guarantee programs allow governments to increase access to capital and invest in businesses, thus promoting redevelopment in their communities.

A loan guarantee program can be a driver for economic development, and encourages public/private partnerships among government, business and the lenders. While the federal government operates two of the most successful guarantee programs, state governments have begun to expand their roles in this area. Numerous loan guarantee programs exist in states throughout the country. Communities with limited resources can take advantage of such programs by marketing them to businesses and partnering with state governments.

Communities with greater financial capacity should consider the creation of a guarantee program that starts off small and grows to a larger capacity. Partnering with lending institutions is one critical aspect of creating a guarantee program.

Linked Deposit Programs

Another valuable set of tools for providing businesses with access to capital are linked deposit programs (LDPs). Linked deposit programs provide businesses with access to affordable capital by offering loans at reduced interest rates. These programs use "linked" state or local deposits to buy down the interest rate.

Once a borrower is approved for a loan, the linked governmental partner will make a deposit with the lender at an amount significant enough to create a lower interest rate on the borrower's loan for a set period of time. The interest rate on the borrower's loan is then usually 2 to 3% lower than the bank's traditional rate. During that period in which the interest rate is below market rate, the lender will pay the linked partner a reduced interest rate on its deposit. In the end, the lender pays less for the deposit than it receives, and thus can charge less for the loan it makes. The borrower is able to pay less interest on the loan, and the linked governmental partner receives less interest on its deposit.

Linked deposit programs are made particularly strong when a variety of lending institutions – such as credit unions, savings banks, commercial banks and other institutions – elect to participate. A wide array of participants create a deeper pool of capital, and thus increase economic activity. Most of the paperwork and credit review is conducted by the lending institution, and this reduces the administrative cost for the linked governmental partner. However, the ultimate eligibility decision lies with the linked governmental partner to ensure that borrowers meet the program criteria.

These programs can be tailored to assist with different types of financing, and they have been adapted for various purposes throughout the country. There are dozens of variations of linked deposit programs, with different rates, deposits, terms and eligibility requirements. Typically, state governments operate these programs, due to their ability to deposit funds with lending institutions. However, some large cities have also employed these structures. To address the needs of distressed neighborhoods, linked deposit programs are often matched with targeted financing tools.

Sources: Ohio Treasure of State, Linked Deposit Programs, www.tos.ohio.gov/index.php/ linked-deposits, 2008
New York State Linked Deposit Program, www.nylovesbiz.com/Tax_and_Financial_ Incentives/Loan_Discounts/default.asp, 2008

Small Business Administration

The U.S. Small Business Administration (SBA) recognizes the important economic role small businesses play in our communities, and the SBA has established various support tools to help small businesses. Through two loan programs, the CDC/504 Loan Program and the 7(a) Loan Program, the SBA provides small business owners with access to financing that might not be available through conventional channels. Historically, however, these programs have been vastly under-utilized.

Certified Development Company (CDC)/504 Loan Program

The SBA 504 Loan Program provides businesses with funding for the purchase of fixed assets such as land, buildings and machinery. 504 loans are funded through Certified Development Companies, which are nonprofit corporations that promote economic development in their communities. In partnership with the SBA and private lenders, CDCs provide financing to small businesses.

Typically, a 504 loan has three funding sources. Generally, a bank contributes up to 50% of the project financing, a CDC supplies up to 40%, and the small business contributes at least 10%. The bank and the CDC each make a separate loan to the qualifying business.

The loan made by the CDC is backed by a 100% SBA guaranteed debenture. If job creation goals are met, then the maximum SBA debenture will be $1.5 million. Generally, one job must be created or retained for every $50,000 in SBA funding, except in the case of small manufacturers, which must create or retain a job for every $100,000 in SBA funding they receive.

If the project meets a designated public policy goal, then the SBA debenture is expanded to $2 million. Such public policy goals may include: business district revitalization, export expansion, minority business development, rural development, increased productivity and competitiveness, a restructuring due to federally mandated standards or policies, changes that are necessitated by federal budget cutbacks, and expansion of veteran-owned small businesses. The intention of the program is to catalyze economic development in the community, thereby helping to create or retain jobs.

For-profit firms with a net worth of less than $7 million are eligible for this program. These businesses must also have an average two year profit of less than $2.5 million after taxes. If the loan is to be used for a facility, then the business applicant must be the primary user of the facility. There is a minimum of 51% occupancy for existing facilities and 60% for new construction.

For the 504 program, traditional lending institutions typically provide the primary financing, which covers up to 50% of the project cost, while the CDC provides secondary financing. Most of the upfront fees are included with the loan, and processing fees total approximately 2.75%. The program offers lower interest rates than those normally attainable through conventional lending. The SBA loan rate is typically fixed for 20 years, which offers another significant benefit of the program.

Source: U.S. Small Business Administration, www.sba.gov, 2009

7(a) Loan Program

The 7(a) Loan Program, the most popular loan program offered by the SBA, offers guarantees to private sector lenders who finance small businesses. In return, the SBA provides a guarantee of repayment in case of default.

When a lender processes the application, it decides whether or not to make the loan, and if it will require an SBA guarantee. If the lender moves ahead, then it must structure the loan according to SBA requirements, and in return, it receives a guarantee from the SBA for a portion of the loan.

In the event of payment default, the SBA will reimburse the lender for a portion of the loss, but the borrower is obligated to repay the loan amount. The 7(a) program allows lenders to offset some of the risk associated with lending to small businesses, while still ensuring accountability in the event of default.

The eligibility requirements for the 7(a) program are fairly broad, in order to accommodate a diverse array of small business needs. Businesses must meet SBA size standards, and the funds may then be used for machinery and equipment, expansion and renovation, purchasing an existing business, working capital, refinancing, start-up for a new business and many other items.

The maximum loan amount for the 7(a) program is $2 million. The SBA's exposure is limited to $1.5 million, with a maximum guarantee of 75%. The borrower and lender typically negotiate rates, which may be fixed or variable. To offset taxpayer costs, the lender is charged a guarantee fee and a servicing fee for each loan. Such fees are based on the guaranteed portion of the loan; the borrower is charged an upfront guarantee fee, while the lender pays a fee to the SBA. Such fees vary depending on the size of the loan.

Source: U.S. Small Business Administration, www.sba.gov, 2009

Micro-Enterprise Finance

Capital programs exist to serve the smallest businesses in a community as well. These businesses, often referred to as micro-enterprises, are defined as small businesses with less than five employees, a capital need of less than $35,000, and an average loan amount of $7,000. The Association for Enterprise Opportunity estimates that there are twenty-four million micro-enterprises across the country. These small businesses play a significant role in our economy, employing approximately one of every six private sector employees.

Micro-enterprises require a tailored financing approach, as due to their small size and entrepreneurial nature, they are perceived by lenders as having a high level of risk. The micro-enterprise development industry is strong throughout the country, as the federal government and many finance agencies have developed programs to provide financing and support for these businesses.

SBA Micro-Loan Program

The federal government has played a significant role in supporting micro-enterprises via the Small Business Association's Micro-Loan Program. Under this program, the SBA makes funds available to nonprofit, community based lenders, called intermediaries, and these lenders in turn make loans of up to $35,000 to eligible borrowers. The average loan size for this program is approximately $13,000. Applications are typically submitted to the local intermediary, and credit decisions are made on the local level.

The SBA allows a maximum term of six years for a micro-loan. However, loan terms vary according to the size of the loan, the planned use of funds, the requirements of the intermediary lender, and the needs of the borrower. While interest rates vary depending on the costs that the U.S. Treasury passes on to the intermediary and other factors, these rates generally range between eight and thirteen percent.

Each intermediary lender has its own lending and credit requirements. Intermediaries typically require the personal guarantee of the business owner as well as some type of collateral. Intermediaries are required to provide training and technical assistance to borrowers. When applying for a loan, micro-enterprises may be asked to meet training or planning requirements before their application is considered.

National Science Foundation (NSF) – SBIR & STTR Programs

The National Science Foundation (NSF) is an independent federal agency created by Congress to promote the progress of science, health and national defense. NSF is the funding source for approximately 20 percent of all federally supported basic research conducted by U.S. colleges and universities. In many fields such as mathematics, computer science and the social sciences, NSF is the major source of federal backing. NSF runs the successful Small Business Innovation Research (SBIR) and Small Business Technology Transfer (STTR) programs. Eleven federal departments participate in the SBIR program; five departments participate in the STTR program awarding billions in funding to small high-tech businesses. Both programs provided competitive grants for small business development for high-tech and innovation industry business development.

The NSF website provides detailed program information at www.nsf.gov.

Local Micro-Lending Programs

Many states and communities lend directly to micro-enterprise businesses. This is called micro-lending, and it is typically done through development finance agencies or through partnerships with community-based lending institutions, community development corporations, special development districts, chambers of commerce and other entities. These programs are often tailored to address specific niches such as minority- or women-owned businesses, home-based businesses, or businesses owned and/or operated by people with disabilities.

There are considerable challenges in managing a micro-lending program, including effective program marketing and maintaining the performance of the loan portfolio. Micro-enterprise lending carries more risk than a typical revolving loan fund. Many micro-enterprise businesses are run by individuals who are not familiar with business, financial and strategic planning. Hence, the entity managing a micro-lending program may have to do a certain amount of up-front work, including education, training and technical assistance prior to lending funds to a potential borrower. Development finance agencies that offer micro-lending programs must work diligently to craft a program that is fair and reasonable, and provides a clear set of expectations and deliverables.

Micro-lending program managers should be prepared to manage loan loss and performance issues. They should also be prepared to address these challenges with the partners, funding sources and stakeholders who helped to capitalize the fund. Public/private partnerships between finance agencies and lending institutions require considerable work, but they are worth the effort in the long run.

Marketing these programs can also be a constant challenge, as they are geared towards small businesses that are often less visible. Home based businesses and small consulting firms are good examples of micro-enterprise businesses that may require support, but are difficult to reach.

Peer-Based Micro-Lending

A peer-based program, through which entrepreneurs and other small businesses lend to micro-enterprise businesses, is a unique type of micro-lending. In this case, the peer group acts as the lending institution; members review applications, credit-worthiness and business plans. Upon making a loan, they monitor the loan performance and overall portfolio. This type of program is effective because as micro-enterprise businesses develop and grow, they have the opportunity to become a part of the peer lending group and assist others. As micro-enterprise businesses succeed, they often progress to larger, established financing sources such as loan funds and mezzanine programs.

Source: Karl Seidman, Economic Development Finance, Sage Publications, 2005

Wrapping up Access to Capital Lending Tools

The importance of capital financing tools can hardly be overstated. These tools offer a vital way of assisting the businesses in a community. They play a vital role in opening new markets, strengthening commercial districts and fostering innovation.

Building such capital programs can be daunting. However, development finance agencies should not fear the due diligence and administrative oversight that is required to use these capital tools. Partnerships with private institutions can help local and state governments manage these programs. In addition, many of these programs can be operated by unique agencies, such as CDCs and business associations that develop expertise in program marketing and development and provide effective oversight.

Development finance agencies should embrace and develop capital tool programs. In doing so, they will demonstrate an understanding of local business challenges and the ability to respond to their capital needs.

Understanding Support Tools

Support tools are defined as those that are more flexible, less complex, and more easily applied than most other development finance tools. They also offer gap financing.

Support tools can fit into the category of bedrock tools, targeted tools, capital tools, and investment catalyst tools. They are often used in conjunction with other tools. However, like all development finance tools, support tools are not always readily available, nor are they guaranteed to achieve project success.

Development finance agencies should be aware of the support tools that are available. The availability of such tools depends on the local context. While federal support tools such as CDBG and EDA funding are typically available on an annual basis, various tax incentives and foundation funds may only be available for a set period, or in response to specific financing challenges. Finance agencies should designate a point person to monitor the availability of such funding, and to maximize opportunities to use support tools for project financing.

Support tools exist at every level, from federal economic development programs to local foundation funding. This chapter will cover an array of tools in this category, but due to the proliferation of such tools, the list will not be exhaustive.

Federal Economic Development Financing Agencies & Programs

There are over thirty different federal programs that finance economic development. Many of these programs provide funding directly to a local governments, while others provide funding to a business. Often, these resources supplement local efforts and come in the form of guarantees, loans and grants. The federal government provides billions of dollars annually, and when utilized fully, these resources can make a difference at the local level.

For economic development practitioners, the first part of using support tools effectively is to develop an understanding of available federal programs. Next, practitioners must take advantage of these opportunities and build partnerships with cooperative agencies within the community. There are many different state and local agencies that play a role in the delivery of federal programs. These state and local agencies often employ outreach coordinators and professionals who help build partnerships, provide program education, and assist with funding requests. Economic development practitioners should develop partnerships with these agencies.

Note: As of the writing of this book, these agencies and programs were functioning as described. Information for this chapter was taken from individual federal agencies' websites to ensure accuracy. Due to the nature of federal budgeting and funding availability, this information may be outdated. Check with each agency before attempting to access or implement these programs.

U.S. Department of Housing & Urban Development (HUD)

The U.S. Department of Housing and Urban Development (HUD) is the largest federal agency dedicated to the economic development industry. HUD offers a host of programs to foster community and economic development. These programs include:

- Community Development Block Grant (CDBG)
- Brownfield Economic Development Initiative (BEDI)
- Rural Housing and Economic Development (RHED)

Community Development Block Grant Program (CDBG)

The Community Development Block Grant (CDBG) program is HUD's flagship program. The CDBG program provides resources for communities to address a wide variety of needs. The program attempts to provide services to the most vulnerable in the community, and to ensure that residents have access to affordable housing. Through the CDBG program, HUD provides annual grants to over 1,100 local governments and states based on a formula. Here are some of the CDBG programs:

- Entitlement Communities
- State Administered CDBG
- Section 108 Loan Guarantee Program
- HUD Administered Small Cities
- Insular Areas
- Disaster Recovery Assistance
- Renewal Communities/Empowerment Zones/Enterprise Communities (RC/EZ/EC)

The two main CDBG funding designations are "non-entitlement" and "entitlement" communities. Those communities that receive funding under the "entitlement" funding formula are cities located within a Metropolitan Statistical Area (MSA). To qualify as an MSA, the core city must have a population of at least 50,000 and it must be located within an urban county with an additional population of 200,000 or more.

Individual states distribute CDBG funds to local communities that are considered "non-entitlement" communities. The amount of funding that each community receives is based on a formula made up of several indicators, including community need, population, housing density, age of housing stock, population growth in comparison to other communities, and other factors.

Funding can be used for a wide variety of activities, including:

- Acquisition of real property
- Relocation and demolition
- Rehabilitation of residential and non-residential structures
- Construction of public facilities and improvements
- Public services
- Activities related to energy conservation and renewable energy sources
- Assistance to for-profit businesses to carry out economic development and job creation and retention activities

There are also a variety of ineligible activities, and these should be noted by economic development practitioners. HUD staff members are trained to assist communities in meeting submission and program requirements.

As it relates to economic development, there are a few specific CDBG programs that finance agencies can utilize.

- *Section 108 Loan Guarantee Program*
  The Section 108 Loan Guarantee Program provides communities with a source of funding to address economic development, housing rehabilitation, public facilities, and large scale development projects. The Section 108 Loan program allows a community to turn a portion of their CDBG grant funding into a guarantee loan program, which allows a community to commence economic revitalization. The Section 108 Loan Program is paired with two other HUD programs: the Economic Development Initiative (EDI) and the Brownfield Economic Development Initiative.

  The 108 Program allows a community to receive a HUD loan using the community's future CDBG allocation as collateral. The loan can be paid off using a variety of income sources, such as taxes and future CDBG dollars. Loans can be paid off over a period of twenty years, and the terms of the loan are flexible, making this an excellent development tool.

  Because this program subjects a community's future CDBG funding to use as collateral, this is also a risky program. Should the project fail, the community would be forced to use its CDBG funds in order to pay back the loan, thus eliminating the ability to use such funding for other projects over a period of time.

- *Disaster Recovery Assistance Program*
  Communities that have been declared a disaster area are eligible for Disaster Recovery Assistance. Under this HUD program, communities have several options to help them with their recovery efforts, such as redirecting previously awarded grants, expediting grant awards and waiving regulatory program requirements. HUD also works with the Federal Emergency Management Agency (FEMA) and the SBA to expedite recovery assistance.

- *Renewal Communities, Empowerment Zones & Enterprise Communities (RC/EZ/EC)*
  Chapter Four of this book discussed the available financing tools provided by the federal RC, EZ & EC programs. The goal of these programs is to bring communities together through public and private partnerships in order to attract economic and community development investment.

  The Renewal Community (RC) program offers a host of incentives to encourage business development, including tax credits, workforce credits, tax deductions and bond investment incentives. The Empowerment Zones (EZ) and Enterprise Communities (EC) programs are similar to the RC programs. The EZ program targets small and mid-size businesses within a defined geographic area. The EZ and EC programs encourage businesses to open, expand and hire local residents in a targeted area through incentives that include employment tax credits, low-interest loans through bond sale proceeds, and deductions.

Brownfields Economic Development Initiative (BEDI)
HUD's Brownfield Economic Development Initiative (BEDI) provides competitive grants to spur the redevelopment of brownfields. Brownfields are under-utilized industrial or commercial sites at which expansion and redevelopment are hindered by real or perceived environmental contamination. The BEDI program is used in conjunction with the Section 108 Loan Guarantee program. BEDI grants can be used for a variety of financing needs including:

- Land write-downs
- Site remediation costs
- Funding reserves
- Over-collateralizing the Section 108 Loan
- Direct enhancement of the security of the Section 108 Loan
- Providing financing to for-profit businesses at below market interest rate

Rural Housing and Economic Development (RHED)
The purpose of the Rural Housing and Economic Development (RHED) program is to provide grants that address the economic development and housing needs of rural communities. There are a variety of requirements and criteria for communities to consider with this program. Funds are available in two categories:

1.) Capacity building and support for innovative housing and economic development activities that allow organizations to carry out new functions or to perform existing functions more effectively. The maximum award amount is $150,000, and it can be used for hiring and training staff, purchasing software and other tools, obtaining outside expertise, engaging technical assistance, and purchasing or leasing office space.

2.) Support for innovative housing and economic development activities. The maximum award amount is $400,000, and the funds can be used for a narrower list of activities, including preparation of plans and architectural drawings, acquisition of land and buildings, demolition, infrastructure development, the purchase of materials, and construction costs.

HUD's website provides detailed information on these programs at www.hud.gov.

Economic Development Administration (EDA)

The EDA is a federal agency that funds economic development activities. The EDA provides support through a variety of programs that are geared towards innovation and economic development. Here is an overview of those programs.

Public Works Grants

EDA provides annual grants to support the construction or rehabilitation of essential public infrastructure and facilities. These capital infrastructure improvements typically require additional financial assistance and may include brownfield redevelopment.

Planning Program

The Planning Program helps to support planning organizations, including District Organizations and Indian Tribes, in the development, revision and implementation of comprehensive economic development strategies (CEDS). The program also provides grants for related short-term planning investments and state plans designed to address challenges in distressed regions.

Economic Adjustment Assistance Program

The Economic Adjustment Assistance Program provides technical, planning and infrastructure assistance in regions that are experiencing adverse economic change. The program is designed to address major economic change, such as mass layoffs or economic downturns in regions or communities.

Revolving Loan Funds

The EDA also provides grants on an ongoing basis to capitalize revolving loan funds (RLFs). As discussed in previous chapters, these loan funds have a variety of uses, and the EDA is a good source for start-up funding. However, federal funding comes with rules and regulations that must be followed. Loan funds capitalized with EDA grants are subject to numerous restrictions and should be monitored closely by fund administrators.

EDA's website provides detailed information on all of these programs at www.eda.gov.

U.S. Department of Treasury –
Community Development Financial Institutions Fund (CDFI Fund)

The CDFI Fund operates one very important financing program as well as a few lesser known initiatives. The most significant program is the New Markets Tax Credit (NMTC) program, which is covered in Chapter Five. The Fund also operates the Bank Enterprise Award Program, which supports FDIC-insured financial institutions who support community and economic development activities. The program provides financial incentives to institutions that increase lending, investment and services in economically distressed areas.

The CDFI Fund's website provides detailed information on all of these programs at www.cdfifund.gov.

U.S. Department of Agriculture (USDA)

The USDA Rural Development office has a comprehensive set of programs and services that support a wide array of economic development activities.

Business and Industry Guaranteed Loan (B&I) Program

This program provides loan guarantees to organizations, corporations, partnerships, nonprofits and individuals for projects with lasting community impact, including job creation, economic development, water resource development and renewable energy development.

Intermediary Re-lending Program (IRP)

This program provides loans to organizations (called intermediaries) for the creation of revolving loan funds to service rural areas. These intermediaries may be nonprofits or public agencies, and the loans provided by the intermediaries must be used for eligible rural development activities. Eligible uses include: business acquisition and construction, land purchase and development, equipment purchases, working capital and start-up costs, pollution control, transportation services, feasibility studies and hotels, and the development of motels, bed and breakfasts and convention centers.

Rural Business Enterprise Grant (RBEG) Program

The RBEG program provides grants for rural projects that aid in developing small businesses, distance learning networks, and employment training programs. Rural communities, public entities and nonprofits are eligible.

Rural Business Opportunity Grant (RBOG) Program

The RBOG program provides grants for sustainable economic development initiatives focusing on training and technical assistance for business development, entrepreneurs, and economic development officials, as well as assistance with economic development planning. Public entities and nonprofit organizations are eligible for grants up to a maximum of $50,000 for single states.

Rural Economic Development Loan and Grant (REDLG)

The REDLG program provides funding to rural projects through local utilities. Under the REDLG program, USDA provides zero percent interest loans to local utilities, and these utilities in turn provide discounted funding to local businesses for projects that create and retain employment. The recipients repay the lending utility directly, and the utility is responsible for repayment to the USDA.

Under the REDLG program, the USDA also provides grants to local utilities that use their grant money to establish revolving loan funds. The utilities make loans from the fund to help create or retain jobs in rural areas. When the fund is terminated, the grant is repaid to the USDA.

Rural Energy for America Program Grant (REAP Grants)
REAP Grant provides grants for energy audits and renewable energy development. It also provides funds to agricultural producers and rural small businesses to purchase and install renewable energy systems and to make energy-efficiency improvements.

Rural Energy for America Program Guaranteed Loan Program (REAP Loans)
The REAP guaranteed loan program encourages the commercial financing of renewable energy (bio-energy, geothermal, hydrogen, solar, and wind) as well as energy efficiency projects. Under the program, project developers work with local lenders, who in turn apply to USDA Rural Development for a loan guarantee of up to 85 percent of the loan amount.

Other USDA Programs
USDA has a number of community development and agricultural business development support programs. These programs include:

- **Army Armament Retooling & Manufacturing Support (ARMS) Program –** Offers commercial and industrial businesses the opportunity to establish business centers at eligible Army production facilities.

- **Biobased Products and Bioenergy Program (BIOMASS) –** Finances technologies that are needed to convert biomass into bio-based products and bio-energy in a manner that is cost-competitive in large national and international markets. Loans for biomass conversion into bio-based products and bio-energy are eligible for financing under the Business and Industry Guaranteed Loan Programs.

- **Community Adjustment and Investment Program (CAIP) –** Through the North American Development Bank (NADBank), this program lends to businesses in communities with significant levels of workers adversely impacted by NAFTA-related trade.

- **Agriculture Innovation Center (AIC) Program –** Funds grants made to innovation centers that provide technical and business development assistance to agricultural producers who seek to engage in marketing value-added products.

The USDA Rural Development website provides detailed information on all of these programs at www.rurdev.usda.gov.

U.S. Small Business Administration (SBA)
The SBA provides a variety of financing options, including the 504 Loan Program, 7(a) Loan Program and the Microloan Program, all of which are discussed in more detail in Chapter 6.

The SBA website provides detailed information on all of these programs at www.sba.gov.

Environmental Protection Agency (EPA)
The U.S. EPA is the lead federal agency that addresses the nation's environmental science, research, education and assessment issues. The agency's mission is to protect human health and the environment, and through various programs, the agency impacts local development efforts. The EPA primarily helps economic development efforts through brownfields programs that assist with assessment, clean up, job training and tax credits. Over the past decade, EPA funding has provided significant financial assistance for brownfield redevelopment, yielding positive results nationwide. The EPA's programs are some of the most successful and significant in the federal government's approach to economic development. Some of the EPA's programs include:

Assessment Grants
Assessment grants provide funding to inventory, characterize, assess, and conduct planning and community involvement related to brownfield sites. An eligible entity may apply for up to $200,000 to assess a site contaminated by hazardous substances, pollutants or contaminants (including hazardous substances co-mingled with petroleum). Applicants may seek a waiver of the $200,000 limit and request up to $350,000 for a site that is contaminated by hazardous substances, pollutants, or contaminants. Applicants may seek up to $350,000 to assess a site contaminated by petroleum, and up to $200,000 to address the petroleum contamination. Such waivers must be based on the anticipated level of hazardous substances, pollutants, or contaminants (including hazardous substances co-mingled with petroleum) at a single site. Total grant fund requests should not exceed $400,000 unless a waiver is requested. Due to budget limitations, no entity may apply for more than $700,000 in assessment funding. The performance period for these grants is two years.

Revolving Loan Fund Grants
The EPA has provided states (including U.S. territories), political subdivisions (including cities, towns, and counties), and Indian tribes with grants to capitalize the Brownfields Cleanup Revolving Loan Fund (BCRLF). The purpose of this loan fund is to make low interest loans for the purpose of cleaning up brownfields. Use of BCRLF loan funds is limited to brownfields that have been determined to have an actual release or substantial threat of release of a hazardous substance. Loans may also be used at sites with a release or substantial threat of release of a pollutant or contaminant with an imminent or substantial danger to public health and welfare. Nearly 120 entities have been awarded grants to start up BCRLFs since the program's inception. These entities are listed on the EPA website.

Cleanup Grants
Cleanup grants provide funding for a grant recipient to carry out cleanup activities at brownfield sites. An eligible entity may apply for up to $200,000 per site. These funds may be used to address sites contaminated by petroleum and hazardous substances, pollutants, or contaminants (including hazardous

substances co-mingled with petroleum). Cleanup grants require a twenty percent cost share, which may be a contribution of money, labor, material or services. The cost share must be for eligible costs, cannot include administrative costs, and must equal twenty percent of the amount of EPA funding. A cleanup grant applicant may request a waiver of the twenty percent cost share requirement based on hardship. An applicant must own the site for which they are requesting funding at the time of the application, or demonstrate the ability to acquire title to the property. The performance period for these grants is two years.

Brownfield Tax Incentive
Detailed information on the EPA Brownfield Tax Incentive program is provided in Chapter 5 of this guide.

The EPA's website provides detailed information about all of these programs at www.epa.gov/brownfields.

U.S. Department of the Interior (DOI) – National Park Services
The DOI is in charge of managing the Federal Historic Preservation Tax Incentives program through the National Park Service and the Internal Revenue Service (IRS). This program is covered in depth in Chapter 5 of this publication. Rehabilitation tax credits were established in order to discourage the unnecessary demolition of older buildings and to slow capital flight from older urban areas. This type of incentive offers a credit against the total federal taxes that are owed, and this credit is taken for the year in which the renovated building is "put into service" or completed. Historic rehabilitation tax credits are popular and widely used. In recent years, states such as Virginia and Ohio have created programs that are complementary to this federal program.

The DOI website provides detailed program information at www.nps.gov/history/hps/tps/tax/index.htm.

U.S. Department of Justice (DOJ)
The DOJ administers the creative Weed and Seed initiative, a community-based, comprehensive, multi-agency approach to law enforcement, crime prevention and community revitalization. The Community Capacity Development Office (CCDO) oversees the initiative, which is a strategic approach to preventing and reducing violent crime, drug abuse and gang activity in designated high-crime neighborhoods. There are more than 250 designated Weed and Seed sites throughout the country, located in both large cities and small towns.

The strategy involves a two-pronged approach – law enforcement agencies and prosecutors cooperate in "weeding out" violent criminals and drug abusers, and public agencies and community-based private organizations collaborate to "seed" much-needed human services in these areas. These services can include prevention, intervention, treatment, and neighborhood restoration. A community-oriented policing component can bridge the "weeding" and "seeding" elements.

The U.S. Attorney's Office plays a leadership role in organizing local officials, community representatives, and other key stakeholders to form a steering committee and to allocate resources. The prevention, intervention, and treatment concentrates an array of human services and links law enforcement, social service agencies, the private sector and the community to improve the quality of services to residents. Coordinated neighborhood restoration strategies focus on economic development, employment opportunities, and improvements to the housing stock and physical environment of the neighborhood.

While this is not a direct financing source, this support tool can be used to prepare neighborhoods that are witnessing new investment and the potential for economic growth. Communities interested in becoming a Weed and Seed Community should review the resources provided online by the Department of Justice Community Capacity Development Office.

The DOJ website provides detailed information about this program at www.ojp.usdoj.gov/ccdo/ws/welcome.html.

National Science Foundation (NSF) – SBIR & STTR Programs

The National Science Foundation (NSF) is an independent federal agency created by Congress to promote the progress of science, health and national defense. NSF is the funding source for approximately 20 percent of all federally supported basic research conducted by U.S. colleges and universities. In many fields such as mathematics, computer science and the social sciences, NSF is the major source of federal backing. NSF runs the successful Small Business Innovation Research (SBIR) and Small Business Technology Transfer (STTR) programs. Eleven federal departments participate in the SBIR program; five departments participate in the STTR program awarding billions in funding to small high-tech businesses. Both programs provided competitive grants for small business development for high-tech and innovation industry business development.

The NSF website provides detailed program information at www.nsf.gov.

Export Import Bank of the United States (Ex-Im Bank)

A unique source of support for import and export capacity development comes from the Ex-Im Bank. The bank provides working capital guarantees (pre-export financing), export credit insurance, and loan guarantees and direct loans (buyer financing) through a variety of programs. Communities that are seeking to expand importing and exporting activities should employ these programs as a part of their financing toolbox.

The Ex-Im Bank's website provides detailed program information at www.exim.gov.

Tax Abatements

Perhaps the most popular support tool is tax abatement. This tool eliminates or reduces tax liabilities for qualified projects, investments or other business activities. Tax abatement programs exist in almost every state and local government. These programs are often authorized at the state level and implemented at the local level. In many situations, there are duplicate programs existing at the state and local levels, in order to maximize tax abatement opportunities. This depends on the tax structure in a particular state.

Tax abatements are an indirect financing tool that removes a particular tax liability from a business or individual balance sheet. All businesses pay taxes at the local, state and federal level. Taxes include income, property, payroll, corporate, wage, sales, and other forms of both real and personal property taxation. Each of these taxes is an expense incurred by a business, or individual and it must be accounted for each year.

While it is generally agreed that taxes are necessary, tax abatement programs exist to provide incentive for businesses to expand, invest or relocate in local communities.

In a traditional tax abatement program, a business agrees to make a significant investment in return for the elimination or reduction of certain taxes for a set period of years. Typically, tax abatement agreements may extend up to ten years, but can also be extended beyond this period. Significant investment can be in the form of job creation, physical development, capital investment, research expenditures or other commitments. Most abatement agreements require job creation and capital investment commitments on the part of the business, and in return, offer abatement or reduction of designated taxes.

Abatement agreements come in a variety of forms, from simple documentation completed online, to more complex deals negotiated over a period of time. Depending on the state or local abatement program, the type of tax abatement may vary. In some cases, a variety of taxes may be abated, but doing so may require approval from the taxing authorities whose taxes will be forgone, such as the state, the local county or the school district. Further, some of these abatement agreements will require the business to repay, sometimes on a sliding scale basis, the tax abatement received in the event that the business fails to perform certain related economic development commitments (i.e. minimum job creation commitments, investment levels, etc.). These provisions are commonly referred to as "clawbacks" and should be part of any abatement agreement.

Pros & Cons of Tax Abatements

The general use of tax abatement programs has grown steadily in recent decades, as nearly each and every development finance agency employs this tool. However, abatements have both pros and cons and have been heavily abused. This abuse has subsided in recent years, however, as state and local leaders have implemented stronger performance measures and standards.

A business' ability to save money by not having to pay certain taxes, which in many cases can exceed millions of dollars annually, is the fundamental strength of abatement programs. By not having to pay these taxes, the business is able to save money that is thus funneled back into expansion, relocation or direct investment in such things as machinery, equipment, inventory, research and development.

In many states, the ability to abate taxes is a major driver for business relocations, because this incentive plays a critical role in the competitive site selection process. In other communities, abatements are used to foster investment in under-served neighborhoods, or areas where certain types of business, such as industrial parks and technology incubators, are sought. In general, when administered properly, tax abatement programs can provide significant financial support for project completion.

When abatement programs are abused, it is often easy to detect. Typically, abuse occurs when a community does not conduct a proper "but for" test when evaluating the necessity of the abatements, and when proper oversight is not conducted for monitoring performance under existing agreements. Abuses occur in areas where due diligence and accountability are diminished. Problematic agreements can erode a local tax base quickly.

Employing the "but for" test in abatement deals is a common sense approach to ensuring program and project success. The "but for" test answers the question, "But for the abatement, would the benefited business proceed with the project?" This test mandates that the business offer proof that the project would not come to fruition without abatement, and this proof should be tested against financial analysis.

Agencies that employ the "but for" test consistently will see strong results, greater community buy-in, and less difficulty as the agreement matures. Those agencies that do not use this test open themselves up to criticism, financial failure and community distrust. Models of best practices for conducting the "but for" test exist throughout the country, and are often outlined clearly in program guidelines.

The most common challenge in tax abatement deals is the failure of a business to fulfill its end of the agreement. In such cases, finance agencies must be responsive and flexible to address project pitfalls and the community's fiscal health. The finance agency may need to reach determinations as to whether the failure or default on the part of the business was a function of economic conditions or an intentional act on the part of the business to allocate its resources to a different community. Many states have statutory requirements mandating an annual review of performance by businesses under theses agreements.

These reviews are typically conducted by a tax incentive review council (TIRC) that gathers several times per year to review agreements, to make recommendations for agreement modifications or withdrawals, and to craft policies and guidelines for program development. Employing a review council is a best practice that should be employed by every development finance agency responsible for tax abatement programs.

Wrapping Up Support Tools

Support tools can play a pivotal role in catalyzing new, innovative projects in a community. Support tool programs should be a part of the economic development finance toolbox because they can help practitioners achieve their goals and objectives. Engaging the federal agencies involved in these programs will strengthen these economic development efforts.

Implementing the Development Finance Toolbox

Keys to Toolbox Success

Putting the Development Finance Toolbox in place is a comprehensive effort involving bold thinking, innovative planning, considerable strategizing and a fully supported, cooperative effort from all involved. Agencies that fail to build partnerships and cooperative effort typically fail to implement key aspects of the toolbox for a variety of reasons. Resistance to the toolbox approach will likely exist early in the program planning stages, but once the concept is fully understood, it should be embraced throughout the community.

Keep in mind that not all agencies will manage each of the toolbox elements inside the agency. The toolbox approach brings a myriad of stakeholders to the table providing many different programs. In fact, some of the most successful agencies, such as those featured in the following case studies, have partnerships reaching throughout the community to deliver these programs. These partners may exist at the local, county, regional, state and federal level and should all be part of the toolbox.

Sharing Risk, Credit & Expenses

An important element of the development finance toolbox is the ability to spread risk and credit and to share the expenses of running programs. Very few development finance agencies are able or willing to accept all of the risk involved in financing business and industry. And, fewer have the financial resources to absorb the operating costs of all of these programs.

Conversely, support agencies, such as community development corporations and port authorities, can play a pivotal role in financing specific development needs and have fee structures that allow them to complete these transactions.

The private sector should also be considered a risk and credit sharing partner. The private sector is an eager and willing participant in the development finance toolbox, and they provide a far greater depth of risk ability then other partners. Private sector entities such as banks, thrifts, credit unions, syndicators, equity investors, business coalitions and other private participants all provide opportunities for partnership. In fact, some state and federal laws, such as the Community Reinvestment Act (CRA), mandate that financial institutions make certain amounts of investment in low-income or designated communities. These regulations should be used as part of the process to engage private institutions in the toolbox approach.

The private sector can also address the expenses of running programs, such as revolving loan funds or mezzanine funds. Revolving loan fund banking partners are typically willing to provide loan processing, review and closing services if partnering loans are banked in their institutions. This provides finance agencies with a great support system and a means to catalyze business financing, while also providing a steady stream of growing businesses, and potential clients, for the banking partner.

Build an Adequate Fee Structure

One of the most difficult aspects of the development finance process is the administration and utilization of fees for financing services. Simply put, it costs money to make money, and this holds true for both the public and private sector. Finance agencies that adhere to a reasonable but strict fee structure for their services are able to provide a higher level of service over agencies that do not require these considerations. The private institutions involved in the bond, tax credit, lending, investment and other financing programs highlighted in this guide all accept a high level of risk while also accepting a justifiable level of fees for their services. Finance agencies must develop this same mentality and be willing to impose appropriate fees for the use and access to precious public financing resources.

Education is Critical

While it should go without saying, education is the key to building and utilizing the development finance toolbox. The number one reason that agencies cite for not utilizing specific financing tools is a general lack of understanding of a complex tool. Development finance is complex, perhaps overly complex in some instances, and it requires a full understanding from beginning to end to fully employ the variety of tools available. Bonds represent the bedrock financing concepts that have catalyzed a large percentage of the build environment, while newer tools, such as tax credits, have become the primary force driving investment in low-income communities. While both are critical to economic development, one does not outshine the other, and both should be fully understood and utilized.

A variety of training opportunities exist for one to understand the resources available in the development finance toolbox. Organizations, such as CDFA, provide training that should be encouraged and enforced by agency leadership. The top agencies in the country dedicate specific resources to building a strong staff with expertise in the toolbox programs.

Development Finance TOOLBOX Partnerships

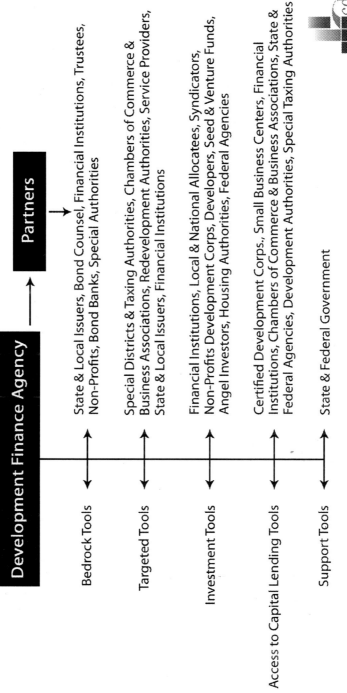

Development Finance Agency → **Partners**

Bedrock Tools → State & Local Issuers, Bond Counsel, Financial Institutions, Trustees, Non-Profits, Bond Banks, Special Authorities

Targeted Tools → Special Districts & Taxing Authorities, Chambers of Commerce & Business Associations, Redevelopment Authorities, Service Providers, State & Local Issuers, Financial Institutions

Investment Tools → Financial Institutions, Local & National Allocatees, Syndicators, Non-Profits Development Corps, Developers, Seed & Venture Funds, Angel Investors, Housing Authorities, Federal Agencies

Access to Capital Lending Tools → Certified Development Corps., Small Business Centers, Financial Institutions, Chambers of Commerce & Business Associations, State & Federal Agencies, Development Authorities, Special Taxing Authorities

Support Tools → State & Federal Government

Note: *This illustration is just an example of the potential partnerships that agencies should build when utilizing the development finance toolbox. Every state has a variety of additional stakeholders that operate unique programs and provide innovative financing tools.*

10 KEY
Development Finance Toolbox Concepts

Understand Development Finance & the Financing Spectrum

1

Build a Development Finance Toolbox Strategy
with Supporting Public Policy Goals

2

Bonds are the Bedrock of Finance

3

Targeted Tools Help Direct Public Investment

4

Investment Tools Cover a Wide Range of Financing Opportunities

5

Access to Capital Lending Tools Finance
Underserved Markets & Growth Industries

6

Support Tools Supplement Financing Efforts

7

Development Finance Toolbox Education is Essential

8

Tool Combinations & Creativity Make the Difference

9

Public & Private Sector Partnerships are Critical

10

From the *Practitioner's Guide to Economic Development Finance*

TOOLBOX CASE STUDIES

Toolbox Case Studies

The following ten case studies represent just a few of the many finance agencies utilizing the development finance toolbox approach. While each of these agencies is unique and represents very different geographic, economic and social demographics, they all understand the importance of employing a comprehensive approach to address business, industry and real estate finance.

These agencies should be seen as models for development agencies seeking to employ the toolbox approach. One critical element to consider with each agency is the high level of partnership and cooperation they all embody. Each of these agencies is on the innovative cutting edge of development finance because they have invested in program development, staff education, policy creation, partnerships and a spirit of shared success throughout the community.

1. City of Minneapolis Department of Community Planning and Economic Development

2. Atlanta Development Authority

3. City/County of Denver Office of Economic Development, Denver Urban Redevelopment Authority

4. Allegheny County Economic Development

5. St. Louis County Economic Council

6. Chester County Economic Development Council

7. New Jersey Economic Development Authority

8. MassDevelopment

9. Arkansas Development Finance Authority

10. Oregon Economic and Community Development Department

CITY OF MINNEAPOLIS DEPARTMENT OF COMMUNITY PLANNING AND ECONOMIC DEVELOPMENT

About the Agency

The City of Minneapolis Department of Community Planning and Economic Development (CPED) is charged with creating growth and promoting sustainability. CPED's authority crosses into a number of areas including housing, community development, business development, planning, and employment education and training.

Structure

CPED has three divisions: Economic Development, Planning, and Housing Development. From the perspective of economic development finance, the Economic Development Division carries out the majority of applicable programs and functions.

The Economic Development Division also has three sections: Business Development, Business Finance and Employment and Training. The Business Finance and Business Development sections are responsible for implementing and managing CPED's economic development finance programs.

CPED also works with and on the behalf of Hennepin County on many financing programs.

How They Utilize the Development Finance Toolbox

CPED's programs accent different types of bond finance and revolving loan funds. CPED can issue IDBs, revenue bonds, tax-exempt, bank qualified, and other bonds. They also have a variety of loan funds to meet the needs of businesses of all types and sizes and have utilized federal incentive programs, such as the Enterprise Zone and New Markets Tax Credits.

Bedrock Tools	**Revenue Bond Program** • Revenue bonds may be used to finance industrial, commercial and medical facilities, multifamily rental housing, nursing homes and some nonprofit activities. • Revenue bonds are issued either free-standing or through the Minneapolis Common Bond Fund (CBF).

Bedrock Tools *(continued)*	**Common Bond Fund Revenue Bond Program (CBF)**

Common Bond Fund Revenue Bond Program (CBF)

- The CBF is a loan fund for growing manufacturing companies. Most of the major manufacturing projects completed in Minneapolis since 1982 have been financed with tax-exempt or taxable revenue bonds issued through the CBF.

- The CBF is designed for established owner-occupied manufacturing facilities with a history of profitability, whose owners provide personal guarantees.

Bank Qualified Bank Direct Tax-Exempt Loan Program

- This financing program provides cost-effective tax-exempt financing for capital projects for smaller 501(c)(3) organizations for projects in the $1 million to $2 million range for which a traditional revenue bond is not practical.

- The streamlined application and documentation process results in reduced borrowing costs and an expedited approval process.

Access to Capital Lending Tools

Business Development Fund (BDF)

- The BDF is a financial tool provided to Minneapolis-based businesses for assistance in redevelopment projects that have the potential to create jobs that will be filled by Minneapolis residents.

- The BDF provides loans of up to $75,000 to Minneapolis businesses and the opportunity for prepayment credits to be earned for each Minneapolis resident hired (during the first three years of the loan) and employed at least one year.

Capital Acquisition Loan Program

- This program enables small business owners to purchase and rehabilitate small commercial and industrial properties.

- The City of Minneapolis, in tandem with private banks, provides financing for projects of up to approximately $1 million. The lender finances at least 50% of the project, the City finances up to 40%, and the business borrower provides the remaining funds in the form of equity.

Two-Percent Loan Program

- Two-Percent Loan program provides financing to small Minneapolis businesses (retail, service or light manufacturing) to purchase equipment and/or to make building improvements. A private lender provides half the loan at market rate and the City provides the rest at 2% interest.

- Loan maximums are $50,000 and $75,000 for businesses in designated Commercial Corridors and Commercial Nodes.

- Eligible businesses are those that benefit low-to-moderate income persons by creating jobs or improving services.

**Support
Tools**

Minneapolis Empowerment Zone
- CPED is responsible for administering the Minneapolis EZ created by the federal government in 1999.

Web Address   www.ci.minneapolis.mn.us/cped

ATLANTA DEVELOPMENT AUTHORITY

About the Agency

The Atlanta Development Authority was formed in 1997 as a State of Georgia registered local government authority. As the economic development agency for the city, ADA represents in-town Atlanta, which has a population of 525,000 and growing. A research-based economic development organization, it focuses on residential, business and investment growth in the city as outlined in the New Century Economic Development Plan adopted by Mayor Shirley Franklin in 2004. ADA is governed by a nine-member board of directors chaired by the mayor of Atlanta. It has 45 employees and partners regularly with more than 50 economic development partner organizations.

Structure

ADA has six divisions: Commerce and Entrepreneurship; Finance, Facilities and Asset Management; Housing Finance; Legal; Marketing and Public Relations; and Tax Allocation Districts.

How They Utilize the Development Finance Toolbox

ADA fully utilizes the economic development finance toolbox, including bond finance, revolving loan funds, TIFs and tax credits. For the purposes of this case study, only the economic development programs will be outlined. However, ADA also operates many housing programs, including tax-exempt multifamily and single-family bonds, a $75 million Housing Opportunity Bond Fund, and the BeltLine Affordable Housing Trust Fund.

Bedrock Tools	**Revenue Bond Program** • ADA issues industrial development bonds (IDBs) for small and mid-sized manufacturers. • Private activity bonds may be issued to finance property of Section 501(c)(3) nonprofit organizations, such as qualifying schools, charities and healthcare facilities. Some tax-exempt private activity bonds for Section 501(c)(3) organizations can be designated as "qualified" for purchase by banks with full tax benefits.

Bedrock Tools
(continued)

- Private activity bonds also may be issued to finance certain "exempt" facilities and qualifying projects, such as solid waste disposal facilities, hazardous waste facilities, water furnishing facilities, sewage facilities, certain local electric energy facilities, certain local heating or cooling facilities and mass transportation facilities. Airport, dock, wharf and mass-commuting facilities also fall into this category of "exempt" facilities. Although these types of facilities may be leased to private businesses, they must be owned by a governmental unit.

- Lease-purchase bonds are a type of private activity bond that provides a reduction of the ad valorem taxes assessed on real and personal property. This happens indirectly, through the transfer of title of the real and personal property subject to taxation to a development authority and subsequent leasing of the property back from the authority.

Access to Capital Lending Tools

Opportunity Loan Fund
- This program is intended to stimulate job creation in the city of Atlanta. The fund provides gap financing to assist small- and medium-sized businesses that create at least five new jobs in the city of Atlanta.

- Special consideration is given to employers in the six development priority areas designated in Atlanta's New Century Economic Development Plan.

- ADA provides loans of $100,000-$200,000 at an interest rate of one-half of the current prime interest rate plus 2%, with a minimum rate of 4%.

- The Opportunity Loan Fund typically funds 50% of costs, with the other 50% coming from private sources, including capital investment by the borrowers or others, financing from private entities and/or SBA-affiliated loan programs.

SBA 504 Loan Program
- ADA provides financial and technical assistance to small minority- and female-owned businesses to expand and/or relocate in the city. The SBA-504 Loan Program offers businesses a unique source for 90% of their financing. Loans are available through certified development companies certified under the U. S. Small Business Administration 504 Certified Development Corporation Program.

- Loans may be up to $1.5 million or 40% of total project costs (up to $2 million if the company meets a public policy goal). 504 loans for "small manufacturers" may be made up to $4 million.

Access to Capital Lending Tools *(continued)*	**Business Improvement Loan Fund (BILF)**

Business Improvement Loan Fund (BILF)
- The BILF is designed to encourage the revitalization of targeted business improvement districts in the city and to support commercial and industrial development in other eligible areas.

- Two forms of financial assistance are available through the BILF: direct loans and loan participants.

The Phoenix Fund
- The Phoenix Fund assists small- and medium-sized businesses with obtaining affordable loans. It provides financial assistance for the construction and renovation of privately-owed commercial buildings, equipment purchases needed to operate a business, and, in some cases, working capital.

- ADA provides loans of $10,000 to $100,000 at a rate below prime as a way to create and retain jobs for low- and moderate-income residents in the City of Atlanta.

- The project must create or retain one job for each $15,000 loaned, and 51% of jobs must be made available to low- and moderate-income residents.

Targeted Tools
- TIF (referred to as tax allocation districts, or TADs, in Georgia) is used in Atlanta to facilitate the redevelopment of areas that have experienced disinvestment resulting from environmental contamination or blight. ADA offers traditional TIF financing, which utilizes future incremental increases in property taxes generated by new development to fund eligible redevelopment costs through bond or pay-as-you-go financing.

- The use of TADs in redevelopment financing was recently affirmed through a statewide referendum in Georgia allowing each school district to choose whether or not to participate in a TAD.

- ADA has a six-person team dedicated to the planning and implementation of the ten TADs in the City of Atlanta.

- Additional abatement and incentive programs are also available to recruit new businesses through the Commerce and Entrepreneurship department.

Investment Tools

New Markets Tax Credits
- Imagine Downtown, Inc. CDE ("IDI") is a community development entity created by ADA and Central Atlanta Progress to receive and invest New Markets Tax Credits in Downtown

Investment Tools

Investment Tools *(continued)*

and select commercial corridors. IDI was awarded a $60 million allocation of New Markets Tax Credits in 2007 and a $20 million allocation in 2008.

- IDI utilizes New Markets Tax Credits in two primary ways to spur implementation of the Imagine Downtown Plan and improve the economic vitality of Atlanta. First, IDI couples New Markets Tax Credit investments with TAD financing for the development of new or revitalization of existing real estate. Second, IDI adds to ADA's current business loan capabilities to ensure that businesses have adequate access to capital for their expansion projects.

Web Address   www.atlantada.com

CITY/COUNTY OF DENVER OFFICE OF ECONOMIC DEVELOPMENT, DENVER URBAN REDEVELOPMENT AUTHORITY

About the Agency

Denver is a consolidated city/county government. As such, it has both an office of Economic Development, which concentrates on county/region economic issues, and an Urban Redevelopment Authority concentrated on inner-city redevelopment and the prevention/removal of blighted areas. Denver has also been a leader in pursuing green development, cultural development and transit-oriented development.

Structure

Denver's Office of Economic Development (OED) reports directly to the Mayor and coordinates redevelopment strategies with the Denver Urban Renewal Authority (DURA).

OED and DURA work closely with a number of public and quasi-public agencies, including: the Small Business Administration, Colorado Housing and Finance Authority, Seedco Financial Services, Workforce Development Agencies, Community Development Corporations, Micro-Enterprise lenders, and commercial banks, in an effort to create jobs and business opportunities for residents and expand Denver's tax base.

How They Utilize the Development Finance Toolbox

OED and DURA use a variety of tools for financing development. OED focuses on operating Denver's RLF and administering EZ and NMTC programs. DURA analyzes and recommends TIF financing for projects in targeted urban areas as well as financing residential and commercial/retail development in underserved areas.

Bedrock Tools	**Industrial Development Revenue Bonds** • The city of Denver offers a financing mechanism called Industrial Development Revenue Bonds (IDRB) to qualified manufacturing companies. IDRBs are tax-exempt debt obligations issued by the city of Denver to attract and foster the expansion of local manufacturing companies.
Targeted Tools	• DURA is responsible for administering the TIF financing program in Denver. • TIF is used only when an area or property cannot be redeveloped without public investment and when it meets a public objective.

Investment Tools	**New Markets Tax Credits** • The City of Denver has received an allocation of $40 million of New Markets Tax Credits from the Department of the Treasury. • OED works in partnership with the Colorado Housing and Finance Authority, the Colorado Enterprise Fund and several lenders to use NMTC for spurring investment in targeted districts. **Denver Enterprise Zone** • The Denver Enterprise Zone is a Colorado tax credit program administered by the OED that allows businesses located within a specific geographic area to receive tax credits against their state tax liability. • There are a variety of different tax credits available, including tax credits for new employees, rehabilitation of vacant buildings, job training and purchase of manufacturing equipment.
Access to Capital Lending Tools	**Revolving Loan Fund/Neighborhood Business Revitalization** • This gap financing program works by lending up to 25% of project costs, thereby inducing banks to provide the bulk of the financing for small businesses. • RLF program caters to stimulating job creation and revitalizing under-utilized or deteriorated commercial and industrial properties. Location in a RLF targeted area is one eligibility requirement. • The OED also assists businesses that locate in the RLF target area with the permit process. • City funding is limited to a maximum of $350,000 for each project, with a target of one job created for each $35,000 in RLF loan proceeds. • The Neighborhood Business Revitalization (NBR) program is a similar program designed to increase investment in targeted neighborhoods and older commercial districts. Financing through the NBR program is available for up to 50% of the project's cost.
Support Tools	**Neighborhood Marketplace Initiative** • This initiative uses a very comprehensive approach to helping small businesses in Denver's various neighborhood business districts. In addition to utilizing the aforementioned financing tools for small business and real estate development, OED provides market research, public improvements, business development specialists, and other resources to foster the revitalization of neighborhood business areas.
Web Address	www.denvergov.org/DURA

ALLEGHENY COUNTY ECONOMIC DEVELOPMENT

About the Agency

Allegheny County Economic Development (ACED) is the lead economic and residential development agency for Allegheny County, Pennsylvania with offices in Pittsburgh. As the main public financing vehicle for the region, ACED works and collaborates closely with municipalities, councils of governments and nonprofit agencies to prioritize goals and make the best use of available resources.

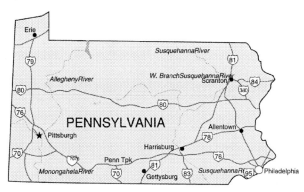

Structure

ACED has eight divisions that each perform separate duties and functions. The divisions are Planning, Business Development, Development, Municipal, Authorities, Operations, Housing and Human Services, and Special Projects and Finance. This case study will focus on the economic development finance tools used by the Authorities, Business Development, Development, and Special Projects and Finance divisions.

The Authorities Division is further divided into the following specialty authorities: Redevelopment Authority of Allegheny County (RAAC), Authority for Improvements in Municipalities (AIM), Allegheny County Industrial Development Authority (ACIDA), Allegheny County Hospital Development Authority (ACHDA), Allegheny County Higher Education and Building Authority (ACHEBA) and Allegheny County Residential Finance Authority (ACRFA). Each Authority specializes in a component of the county's development. Because of their tight focus, the Authorities operate with flexibility and speed in administering bond and loan programs in their designated areas. In 2008, the Authorities Division combined to total over $1.2 billion in bond activity.

How They Utilize the Development Finance Toolbox

With a clear division of authority and areas of expertise, ACED is able to provide diverse loan and bond programs. ACED also creates and uses tax increment financing (TIF) and state and federal grant programs as funding sources.

Bedrock Tools	• ACED utilizes its Authorities to issue tax-exempt and taxable bonds to finance projects in manufacturing, exempt facilities and 501(c)(3) nonprofits. Additionally, through its Authorities, ACED issues bonds to capitalize its first-time home buyer's program and TIF bonds. Finally, ACED issues bank-qualified bonds for smaller transactions done by nonprofits.
Targeted Tools	• The incremental increase in real estate taxes resulting directly from an approved TIF development is used to support a revenue bond issued by a municipal authority created under the Urban Redevelopment Law of Pennsylvania of May 24, 1945. However, the tax increment also includes any tax increase resulting from an increase in commercial activity resulting from the development, including hotel, amusement, business privilege, and parking taxes. • The increment generated by the development may also be used to underwrite a direct loan or another appropriate financing structure. • County policy states, "In any TIF in which the county is a participant, the county's portion of the TIF shall be used only to finance and build the public works infrastructure portion of the project."
Access to Capital Tools	**Allegheny Economic Development Fund (EDF)** • The EDF is designed to assist in the establishment of new industries and the growth of existing businesses to expand the base of taxable properties in Allegheny County. Target sectors include: manufacturing, commercial and commercial services, advanced technology, and retail and retail services. • EDF loans can be secured in three ways: fixed asset financing up to 40% of total eligible project costs not to exceed $100,000, operating funds financing up to 40% of total project costs not to exceed $50,000, fixed asset and operating funds financing combining a maximum of 40% of total project costs not to exceed $100,000, inclusive of operating funds, with operating funds not exceeding $50,000. **Development Action Assistance Program Revolving Loan Fund** • The fund offers low-interest loans to help county businesses grow, create jobs and expand the tax base.

Access to Capital Lending Tools *(continued)*	• Target sectors include manufacturing, commercial/industrial (excluding retail businesses) and advanced technology. Loans are secured with fixed asset financing up to 25% of total eligible project costs not to exceed $500,000.

Allegheny Small Business/Targeted Industry Loan Program

• To promote the establishment and expansion of new and existing businesses by providing low-interest financing for land development, building improvements, machinery and equipment acquisition, infrastructure development, and working capital.

• These programs may be used to finance up to 40% of eligible project costs. Businesses in targeted industries and geographic areas receive lower interest.

Support Tools	• ACED is the lead organization in administering and participating in many state and federal programs. ACED administers the county's Community Development Block Grant (CDBG), HOME and Emergency Shelter Grant (ESG) funds and has been successful in applying for and obtaining grants with the Commonwealth of Pennsylvania and its myriad of grant programs.

Web Address   http://economic.alleghenycounty.us

THE PRACTITIONER'S GUIDE TO ECONOMIC DEVELOPMENT FINANCE

ST. LOUIS COUNTY ECONOMIC COUNCIL

About the Agency
The St. Louis County Economic Council (SLCEC) was formed in 1984 when a handful of smaller agencies came together. SLCEC, a 501(c)(4) organization, is the economic development arm of St. Louis County, and is mandated to drive growth and prosperity in the most economically important county in the state of Missouri.

Over the past 25 years, the Council has grown to provide a broad range of services, with divisions that support small business success, attract and retain corporations, increase the region's international business participation, and revitalize municipalities across the county. SLCEC also plays a significant role in economic development across the greater St. Louis region, working with adjacent economic development agencies.

Structure
SLCEC has six divisions: Real Estate & Community Development Division, World Trade Center Saint Louis, St. Louis Enterprise Centers, Business Finance Division, Center for Business Growth and the Business Development Division. The Business Finance Division administers the bond and loan programs for the county as well as incentive, retention and expansion programs.

How They Utilize the Development Finance Toolbox
SLCEC utilizes the full economic development finance toolbox, including bond finance, revolving loan funds, TIFs and tax credits. They have also successfully coordinated development efforts with surrounding counties and the state of Missouri to maximize impact.

Bedrock Tools	• SLCEC, though the Industrial Development Authority of St. Louis County, offers two options for tax-exempt bond financing for manufacturers based on the amount borrowed. They offer traditional IDB financing for eligible manufacturers on loans between $2 million and $10 million. A mini-bond program for IDBs between $500,000 and $2 million aims to keep costs down for borrowers by reducing fees for bond counsel, trustees and SLCEC. SLCEC also offers traditional and mini-bond programs for 501(c)(3) organizations.

Bedrock Tools *(continued)*	• SLCEC is prohibited under Missouri law from issuing bank-qualified bonds for 501(c)(3) organizations. They have partnered with the Port Authority of St. Louis County to issue these bonds, which often have interest rates 100 basis points lower than traditional tax-exempt financing. • Taxable bonds are also available to companies that do not qualify for tax-exempt financing as manufacturers.
Targeted Tools	• TIF is widely used in Missouri and throughout the region. SLCEC offers traditional TIF financing, which uses increases in real estate taxes to secure and retire bonds. • A Super TIF option is also available in some circumstances, which also captures a portion of the state withholding tax for employees whose jobs were created as part of the project. • Additional abatement and incentive programs are available to recruit new businesses through the Business Development Division.

Access to Capital Lending Tools	**Enterprise Center Revolving Loan Program**
	• This program provides short-term loans (one to five years) to St. Louis Enterprise Center Client Companies to finance a variety of items and needs, such as inventory and working capital.
	• Eligible businesses must be unable to obtain traditional bank or SBA financing.
	
	Brownfields Cleanup Revolving Loan Program
	• This RLF provides gap financing to redevelopment projects or in connection with pre-development activities, with loans ranging from $10,000 to $75,000.
	
	Mezzanine Loan Programs
	• Saint Louis Business Development Fund (SLBDF)
	  – This nationally recognized RLF services the entire St. Louis region (including southwestern Illinois) and will consider investments from $50,000 to $500,000.
	  – Founded in 1994, SLBDF is a for-profit company owned by 24 banks and the three largest economic development agencies in the region. It is professionally managed by SLCEC.
	• Saint Louis Private Fund (SLPF)
	  – Established in 2008, SLPF is a limited liability corporation comprised of 19 individuals who each invested $100,000. SLPF co-invests with SLBDF.

Support Tools

- SLCEC participates in several federal and state zone programs offering different financing and incentive options.

    - Portions of St. Louis County have been designated part of a Federal Empowerment Zone. Companies meeting the federal guidelines of this program in job creation and capital investment may qualify for federal tax credits.

    - The Missouri Enterprise Zone program facilitates relocation and expansion of businesses in economically distressed areas of St. Louis County by offering tax credits and tax abatement related to job creation and capital investment.

    - Portions of St. Louis County participate in the Missouri Rebuilding Communities Program. This program provides tax credits for job creation and capital investment for companies who locate in qualifying communities.

Web Address www.slcec.com

CHESTER COUNTY ECONOMIC DEVELOPMENT COUNCIL

About the Agency

The Chester County Economic Development Council (CCEDC) is a private, not-for-profit economic development organization that has nurtured economic growth in Chester County and the surrounding region for almost 50 years. The purpose of CCEDC is to foster economic development in Chester County and to meet the needs of businesses in the county. With more than 35 federal and state programs available, most businesses (small and large) are eligible to receive funding or other direct business development services through the Council.

Structure

The structure of the CCEDC includes the following divisions: Programs and Services, Government and Municipal Services, Business Development, Internal Financial Services and Loan Programs. The CCEDC is governed by a 50 member volunteer Board of Directors who represent the best interests of the business community, nonprofit organizations, municipalities, education, and public agencies. CCEDC is an IRS approved 501(c)(6) not-for-profit corporation certified by the Commonwealth of Pennsylvania as an Economic Development Corporation. As such, it is one of approximately 55 similar corporations in the state.

How They Utilize the Development Finance Toolbox

The Council's portfolio of business growth services includes low-interest financing, small business lending, workforce training, retention and expansion, customized international business assistance, land and building site selection, brownfields consultation and remediation, urban redevelopment and agricultural economic development. The Council also offers state-of-the art conference and training facilities at its "epicenter" facility in the Eagleview Corporate Center.

Co-located at CCEDC's facilities are over 20 other economic development service providers. Services available through CCEDC's building partners include technology support services, small business consulting and education, customized workforce training, job matching and career transition assistance, and productivity improvement services for manufacturers.

Bedrock Tools	**Tax-Exempt Financing**

Tax-Exempt Financing
- CCEDC offers traditional tax-exempt bond financing in the form of IDBs for manufacturers. They also act as a conduit for nonprofits and exempt facilities (airports, water and sewage plants, solid waste disposal facilities and other federally eligible facilities).

- Loans over $3 million are funded as a stand alone bond issue. A bank can provide a tax-exempt mortgage to the company through the CCIDA for loans under $3 million. Interest earned by the bank is exempt from federal and state taxes. The bank, in turn, passes on a lower interest rate to its borrower.

Access to Capital Lending Tools

Small Business First Fund
- Companies with less than 100 employees from a wide variety of industries may apply for this program, which provides low-cost financing of up to $200,000.

- Except for loans to agricultural producers, one full-time job must be created or preserved within three years of completion of the project for each $25,000 loaned from SBF.

Machinery and Equipment Loan Fund
- This program is available for the acquisition and installation of equipment.

- The maximum loan amount is $5 million or 50% of the purchase, whichever is less.

- Eligible applicants include: manufacturing, biotechnology, mining, information technology, medical facilities and production agriculture.

Next Generation Farmer Loans
- This program uses federal tax-exempt mortgage financing to reduce a farmer's interest rate for capital purchases.

- The program may be used by a borrower and lender for a loan to make a direct purchase of farm and agricultural machinery and equipment or by a buyer and seller for a contract purchase.

- The borrower must not have had any prior direct or indirect ownership interest in a substantial amount of land (19 acres in Chester County) or have a net worth in excess of $500,000.

Access to Capital Lending Tools
(continued)

SBA 504 Loan Program
- CCEDC offers access to SBA 504 loans through the South Eastern Economic Development Corporation of Pennsylvania (SEED Co of PA).

- Federally set guidelines and procedures for the SBA program apply.

Web Address   www.cceconomicdevelopment.com

New Jersey Economic Development Authority

About the Agency

The New Jersey Economic Development Authority (NJEDA) is a self-sustaining state financing and development agency that works to strengthen New Jersey's economy by retaining and growing businesses through financial assistance, by renewing communities, and by promoting the state's strategic advantages to attract domestic and international businesses. NJEDA offers a wide variety of low-interest financing assistance, including tax-exempt and taxable bond financing, loans and loan guarantees, venture capital and business and tax incentives. NJEDA also offers training and technical assistance programs and real estate development assistance.

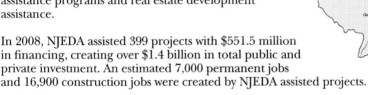

In 2008, NJEDA assisted 399 projects with $551.5 million in financing, creating over $1.4 billion in total public and private investment. An estimated 7,000 permanent jobs and 16,900 construction jobs were created by NJEDA assisted projects.

Structure

The governor appoints members of the NJEDA board and approves NJEDA actions at board meetings. NJEDA does not receive a state appropriation and is self-sustaining. However, under P.L. 2008, c.27, signed in June 2008, certain functions, powers and duties of the New Jersey Commerce Commission were transferred to NJEDA, creating the Division of Business Assistance, Marketing and International Trade within NJEDA. This Division maintains a budget separate from NJEDA, which is funded through annual appropriation by the Legislature from the General Fund.

Although NJEDA is self-supporting, it works closely with the governor to promote the state's economic development policy and goals. The divisions of Business Development and Operations are responsible for directly administering NJEDA's financing programs.

How They Utilize the Development Finance Toolbox

NJEDA utilizes the development finance toolbox through a variety of programs. The largest piece of their program portfolio focuses on low-interest financing assistance, including tax-exempt and taxable bonds, loans and loan guarantees, and venture capital. NJEDA also administers the state's business and tax incentive programs. NJEDA is the primary issuer of industrial development and other private-activity bonds for the state of New Jersey. They also administer the state's tax and business incentives and New Markets Tax Credits program.

Development tools NJEDA uses include the Preferred Lender Program and the Edison Innovation Clean Energy Manufacturing Fund. The Preferred Lender

Program is designed to allow NJEDA to work quickly and easily with private-sector lending partners. NJEDA reviews applications within five days of receipt from a preferred lender to determine if it will participate in and/or guarantee a portion of the bank loan. The Clean Energy Manufacturing Fund was specifically designed to support companies looking to site a Class I renewable energy or energy efficient manufacturing facility in New Jersey.

The newest development tools NJEDA has involve $170 million in financing assistance to help state businesses face fiscal challenges. The funding is made available through two new programs created under Governor Corzine's Economic Assistance and Recovery Plan to stimulate capital investment and job creation. The $120-million InvestNJ program consists of two components. One offers a $3,000 grant to New Jersey businesses for each new job created and retained for one year. The other element of the program authorizes the payment of grants equal to 7% of a business' qualifying capital investment of at least $5,000. The Main Street Business Assistance Program also has two parts: a loan participation and/or guarantee product offered through participating banks, and a line of credit guarantee offered through the NJEDA's 14 Preferred Lender partners.

Bedrock Tools	• NJEDA issues conduit tax-exempt private activity bonds, including IDBs, the proceeds of which are used to provide low-interest, fixed-asset loans. Borrowers must meet the eligibility requirements outlined in the Internal Revenue Code (IRC).
Investment Tools	**New Markets Tax Credits Program** • NMTC program is run in conjunction with the New Jersey Community Development Entity, LLC and provides financing of working capital or fixed assets up to $10 million for qualified businesses and nonprofits. • The project must be located in a distressed area targeted for smart growth. *Many of NJEDA's programs include tax credits as part of a larger package of incentives.*
Access to Capital Lending Tools	**Preferred Lender Program** • In conjunction with its preferred lender banking partners, the NJEDA can provide fixed-asset and working capital loans and loan guarantees. For fixed assets, the maximum NJEDA loan participation is $1.25 million; for working capital, the maximum NJEDA loan participation is $750,000. Maximum guarantees for both categories is $1.5 million.

Access to Capital Lending Tools
(continued)

- Borrowers receive decision within three business days from receipt of complete loan package. Term sheet is issued within two business days of approval.

- Businesses must be New Jersey based, in operation for at least two years, and commit to creating at least one new job per $50,000 in NJEDA exposure. Manufacturers need only to maintain one job per $50,000 of NJEDA exposure.

Direct Loan Program
- Businesses operating in New Jersey that are unable to get sufficient bank credit on their own, with preference given to businesses that are job intensive and located in economically targeted areas or representing a targeted business sector.

- This is "last resort" financing when companies do not qualify for traditional bank loans or other NJEDA programs.

- Up to $1.25 million may be financed for fixed assets or $750,000 for working capital for a term of up to 10 years.

Support Tools

Business Employment Incentive Program
- Economically viable businesses that are expanding or relocating and creating jobs in New Jersey can obtain a grant of up to 80% of the total amount of state income taxes withheld by the company for the new employees hired, awarded for up to 10 years.

- Funds can be used for any business purpose, including the purchase of fixed assets or for working capital to meet operating needs.

- In order to qualify, businesses must create at least 25 new jobs in a 2-year period; emerging technology and biotech companies' eligibility threshold is 10 new jobs.

Urban Targeted Programs
- The Urban Plus Program provides up to $3 million in subordinated financial support to small, woman- or minority-owned businesses, manufacturers, redevelopers and nonprofit organizations in the following endorsed New Jersey municipalities: Camden, Trenton, Newark, Jersey City, Paterson, Elizabeth, East Orange, New Brunswick, and Atlantic City.

- Urban Transit Hub Tax Credit Program was established to stimulate private capital investment, business development and employment by providing state business tax credits for businesses planning a large expansion in or relocation to designated transit hubs in nine New Jersey urban municipalities.

- The Local Development Financing Fund is a revolving loan fund that provides up to $2 million per project for companies located in urban aid municipalities.

Support Tools
(continued)

Edison Innovation Fund Programs

- The Edison Innovation Fund seeks to develop, sustain, and grow technology and life science businesses leading to well paying job opportunities for New Jersey residents through a variety of programs.

- Between October 2006 when the fund was established and January 2009, New Jersey delivered over $338.7 million in financing assistance, venture capital investments, business incentives and tax credits to early-stage and established technology and life sciences businesses. In addition, over $705 million in total project costs was leveraged by these Edison Innovation Fund investments.

Brownfields and Contaminated Site Remediation Program

- Designed for developers in the state of New Jersey in need of financial assistance to clean up and redevelop polluted sites and closed municipal landfills.

- Developer enters into a redevelopment agreement with NJEDA and will be eligible to recover up to 75% of approved costs associated with remediation.

- Eight state taxes, including sales, business use and corporate taxes, may be used to reimburse the developer for remediation costs.

- Developers are required to attend a pre-application meeting with members of NJEDA, the Department of Treasury and the Department of Environmental Protection.

- All work on an approved project must be completed under prevailing wage.

- A Brownfield Redevelopment Loan Program is also available for interim financing to meet remediation costs of a brownfield site. Up to $750,000 over three years may be borrowed at a below-market rate interest rate with a 3% floor.

Web Address   www.njeda.com

MASSDEVELOPMENT

About the Agency

MassDevelopment (or Massachusetts Development Finance Agency), the state's finance and development agency, works with businesses, financial institutions and municipalities to encourage economic growth in the Commonwealth. MassDevelopment is responsible for the management of volume cap and the issuance of IDBs in Massachusetts. However, MassDevelopment's IDB program is just one of the financing and economic development tools the Agency offers. The Agency also provides lending and loan guarantees and real estate development and advisory services.

In its 2007 and 2008 fiscal years, MassDevelopment financed or managed 476 projects statewide representing an investment of more than $5 billion. The Agency closed 30 IDB issues totaling $105 million during this period. In the first 6 months of FY2009, MassDevelopment has closed 11 issues totaling over $40 million.

Structure

MassDevelopment focuses its programs at the local level, with regional offices located throughout the Commonwealth. Each office is staffed by a "client team" which includes a Business Development person (calling on borrowers, lenders and referral sources), a Community Development staff member (for predevelopment finance), an Investment Banker (for bond financing) and a Lender (for direct loans). The regional focus helps the Agency to develop strong relationships with local businesses and nonprofits and to better understand local needs and styles.

The Agency regularly interacts with other state agencies such as the Executive Office of Energy and Environmental Affairs (Department of Energy Resources and Department of Environmental Protection) and the Executive Office of Housing and Economic Development (Department of Business and Technology and Division of Housing and Economic Development). It also works closely with local and regional entities that support economic development. The regional offices work closely with other government agencies and co-locate with the Massachusetts Office of Business Development to facilitate interaction and cooperative calling efforts.

Finally, MassDevelopment's internal marketing staff is responsible for agency-wide marketing and communications strategies, facilitating regular press coverage by regional and national papers and developing regular and special marketing campaigns and product mailings to promote the Agency's various programs.

How They Utilize the Development Finance Toolbox

MassDevelopment utilizes bond financing and a variety of loan and loan guarantee programs. The Agency provides low-cost financing opportunities to businesses and nonprofits for real estate development, working capital, equipment and other needs and works closely with other State and local agencies to deliver its programs.

Bedrock Tools	• Tax-exempt bond financing is available through MassDevelopment and provides low interest rate financing for capital projects. The Agency typically issues about $1 billion a year for diverse purposes.
	• Projects financed must be eligible for tax-exempt financing under the federal tax code, and include 501(c)(3) nonprofit real estate and equipment, municipal and governmental projects, waste recovery and recycling facilities, manufacturing facilities and equipment (IDBs), and affordable residential rental housing.
	• Taxable bond financing is also available for projects and businesses that do not qualify under federal guidelines for tax-exempt financing. This option gives borrowers easier access to capital markets for industrial and commercial real estate projects.
	• The Agency's Capital Financing 501 program provides short-term, tax-exempt commercial paper financing for nonprofit borrowers that can be borrowed and repaid as needed. The one-application process streamlines subsequent loan closings so that borrowers may quickly and efficiently use this program for repeated access to short-term paper.
	• The Agency has also worked with the Department of Energy Resources to structure and issue CREBs for various state facilities and to assist local governments in taking advantage of this program.
	• Most of the Agency's IDBs issued in recent years have been through direct purchases, with more than 60 banks that buy MassDevelopment bonds. The direct purchase program has enabled MassDevelopment to efficiently deliver IDB bond financing for projects as small as $1 million or less.
Access to Capital Lending Tools	• MassDevelopment offers direct loans and loan guarantees to businesses in a variety of industries to promote job growth. They offer low rates and flexible terms and provide technical assistance to maximize opportunities for participating businesses. They specialize in financing complex projects requiring experience and innovative thinking.

**Access to
Capital
Lending
Tools**
(continued)

- Loans may be made directly to borrowers or in participation with local banks. Guarantees are made to local banks to enable them to lend at higher loan to value ratios.

- MassDevelopment's Emerging Technology Fund (ETF) supports innovation and growth in Massachusetts by providing loans and guarantees for technology-based manufacturing facilities and equipment.

- Brownfields Redevelopment Fund offers financing for both assessment and clean-up. Interest-free financing of up to $100,000 is available per project for environmental site assessment, which is unsecured with no interest charged. Financing of up to $500,000 is available for environmental clean-up. Loan terms are flexible and determined on a case-by-case basis. The remediation must be part of a redevelopment project.

Web Address   www.massdevelopment.com

ARKANSAS DEVELOPMENT FINANCE AUTHORITY

About the Agency

The Arkansas Development Finance Authority (ADFA) is the largest multi-purpose issuer of tax-exempt financing in Arkansas. ADFA was formed in 1985 and replaced the previous finance authority that concentrated on housing development. ADFA has retained the former responsibilities of the old authority while adding economic development as a core function.

Structure

ADFA administers funding in the form of taxable and tax-exempt bonds and notes, state general obligation bonds, state tax credits, the administration of private and public grants, and partnering with other state and federal agencies. Funding activities include low to moderate income housing development, small industries, government, education, agricultural business enterprises, and health care. This case study focuses on the economic development programs that ADFA administers.

How They Utilize the Development Finance Toolbox

ADFA is the primary conduit issuer of bond financing in the state and also administers a variety of loan fund and credit enhancement programs. Additionally, ADFA also has a nationally recognized venture capital program.

Bedrock Tools	• ADFA is able to issue a wide variety of taxable and tax-exempt bonds, including IDBs and 501(c)(3) organizations.
	• Industrial Development Bond Guaranty Program
	– In order to allow more companies better access to tax-exempt IDB financing, ADFA has instituted this guaranty program, which takes the place of a line of credit or bond insurance.
	– The guarantee is backed by the Bond Guaranty Reserve Fund. This fund acts as the first source of repayment if the borrower is unable to fulfill its obligations under the contract.
	• ADFA is also the allocating and managing agency for the private activity bond volume cap in the state of Arkansas.

Investment Tools	• Arkansas Institutional Fund (AIF)
	
	   – The AIF is authorized to invest in professionally managed venture capital funds that in turn make risk capital more accessible to promising Arkansas firms.
	
	   – ADFA serves as the contracting entity, provides balance sheet support for the program and is actively engaged in program oversight.
	
	• Risk Capital Matching Fund
	
	   – ADFA is able to provide matching dollars for validation of concept and local angle investment groups

Access to Capital Lending Tools	**Capital Access Program** • This program has been established to make funds available to borrowers who might otherwise be unable to obtain conventional market financing by alleviating some of the risk to the lender. • Participating lending institutions build an earmarked off-balance sheet loan loss reserve account with each loan they enroll in the program. • Contributions to the loan loss reserve fund are paid by the borrower (3%-7%) and matched by ADFA. **Speculative Building Loan Program** • Local industrial development corporations may access this program to finance construction of speculative industrial buildings in their community. • ADFA offers financing up to $1 million to cover up to 80% of the cost of the building at below market rate. **Governmental Finance** • ADFA assists state and local governments with capital improvement projects. **Disadvantaged Business Enterprise Loan Program** • A program to provide working capital loan guarantees to minority contractors who cannot otherwise finance their working capital needs. • Targets any certified DBE contractor. **Tourism Development Loan Program** • This fund offers state loans from $250,000 to $1,000 for business startup or expansion in the tourism industry. • Proceeds must be used for fixed costs and projects are financed as a 50/50 match with a local financial institution.
Web Address	www.arkansas.gov/adfa/

OREGON ECONOMIC AND COMMUNITY DEVELOPMENT DEPARTMENT

About the Agency

The Oregon Economic and Community Development Department (OECDD) works to create, retain, expand, and attract businesses that provide sustainable, living wage jobs for Oregonians through public-private partnerships, leveraged funding, and support of economic opportunities for Oregon companies and entrepreneurs.

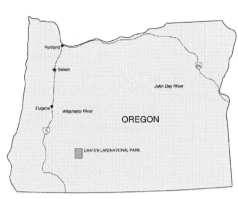

The department provides economic and community development and cultural enhancement throughout the state, and administers programs that assist businesses, communities and people. The Department has a broad mission covering programs and initiatives in many areas. However, this case study will focus primarily on economic development and business finance and incentives.

Structure

Effective as of the first half of 2009, the department consists of four divisions: Policy & Planning, Business Innovation and Trade, Infrastructure Finance and Director's Office.

How They Utilize the Development Finance Toolbox

OECDD uses many aspects of the toolbox. They run a large infrastructure bond program, an Industrial Development Bond with standard and streamlined options, a variety of revolving loan funds, technical assistance programs for Oregon businesses and other incentives.

Bedrock Tools	**Industrial Development Bond Program**
	• Express Bond Program is a streamlined, lower cost option for selling IDBs using standardized documents. The Department uses selected bond counsel with a pre-approved fee schedule. The bonds are placed with the borrower's bank and may be used to finance amounts as small as $1,000,000.
	• Regular IDB Program may utilize either a public offering or private placement. The Regular IDB program will generally provide the greatest economic benefit for borrowers of $5 million or more.

Bedrock Tools *(continued)*	• Both options provide affordable interest rates through tax-exempt bonds to help manufacturers grow. • Program is also available for exempt facilities (docks, solid waste facilities, etc.) and some nonprofits.

Access to Capital Lending Tools

Oregon Capital Access Program
• Program is designed to provide capital for start-up or expansion of small businesses.

• CAP may be utilized for all types of loans and lines of credit.

• Participating lenders build a loan loss reserve each time they enroll a loan. Contributions to the loss reserve account are matched by the state of Oregon.

Oregon Credit Enhancement Fund
• The fund provides guarantees for working capital or fixed asset bank loans and is available for manufacturing, production and processing companies.

• Funds can be used for real property, buildings, machinery and equipment and working capital.

• Focuses on traded-sector businesses; also assists businesses in distressed areas or brownfield sites.

Brownfield Redevelopment Fund
• The fund's primary purpose is to assist private persons and local governments to evaluate, clean up and therefore redevelop brownfields. This program is capitalized by proceeds from the sale of state revenue bonds.

• Any individual, business, nonprofit organization, prospective purchaser, municipality, special district, port or tribe may make application to the Brownfields Redevelopment Fund.

• Environmental actions funded through this program must be linked to site redevelopment that facilitates economic development or community revitalization. Examples of eligible redevelopment projects the program will support include business development projects, industrial lands capacity projects, community facility projects and downtown or mixed use center revitalization projects.

Oregon Business Development Fund (OBDF)
• RLF that provides long-term fixed-rate financing focused on manufacturing, processing or a regionally significant tourist facility. OBDF is targeted for businesses rural and distressed areas. Participants must demonstrate job creation or retention.

Access to Capital Lending Tools *(continued)*	**Entrepreneurial Development Loan Fund (EDLF)** • RLF that provides initial, direct loans to help new businesses. It is designed to fill a niche for microloans to start-ups that traditional lenders do not service. A business must meet two of the following criteria: owned less than 36 months; generated revenues of less than $175,000 in previous 12 months; owned by a severely disabled person. • RLFs are also offered and administered by local authorities/ entities with funding assistance from the Department and the federal government.
Support Tools	**Oregon Business Retention Service** • The program offers companies consulting services delivered by some of the best and most experienced private sector consultants in the state. A consultant is matched with a company based on specific needs and industry requirements. • The maximum benefits are $5,000 for consulting services and $30,000 for feasibility studies, which are to be paid back within two years as an interest-free loan.
Web Address	http://econ.oregon.gov